Battered Women

Battered Women

Micheline Beaudry

Translated by Lorne Huston and Margaret Heap

BLACK ROSE BOOKS   Montréal • Buffalo

920195

Copyright 1985©
Black Rose Books Ltd.

No part of this book may be reproduced or transmitted in any form by means, electronic or mechanical, including photocopying and recording, or by any information storage or retrieval system, without written permission from the author or publisher, except for brief passages quoted by a reviewer in a newspaper or magazine.

Black Rose Books No. N93
ISBN Hardcover 0-920057-47-0
ISBN Paperback 0-920057-46-2

> Canadian Cataloguing in Publication Data
>
> Beaudry, Micheline, 1942-
>   Battered women
>
> Translation of: Les maisons des femmes battues au Québec.
>
> Includes bibliographical references.
> ISBN 0-920057-47-0 (bound).   ISBN 0-920057-46-2 (pbk.).
>
> 1. Abused wives — Services for — Quebec (Province)
> I. Title.
>
> HV6626.B4213 1985   362.8'38'09714   C85-090275-4

Translation of *Les Maisons des femmes battues au Québec*, Editions Saint-Martin, 1984. The publication of this book was made possible with a grant from the Groupe d'analyse des politiques sociales de l'Université de Montréal, which is financially supported by Health and Welfare Canada for professional development in social welfare. "Project no. 4554-19-9"

Cover design: John Sims

Black Rose Books

3981 boul. St. Laurent   University of Toronto Press
Montréal, Qué. H2W 1Y5   33 East Tupper St.
Canada   Buffalo, N.Y. 14230, USA

Printed and bound in Québec, Canada

*For Donald and
for Annie*

Table of Contents

Acknowledgements
Introduction 13

1. Shelters: A Women's Story 17

    Forgotten beginnings 17
    Women organize in a network 22
    The government takes charge 25

2. The Emergence of Women's Houses 29

    Choosing the battleground: the house 29
    An alternative to loneliness 30
    Rejecting the house as a symbol of women's duty 31
    For the liberation of a women's house 33
    The houses as they were founded 35
    A women's house 35
    An emerging response to a real need 36
    The house as a public forum 37
    Institutional counter-productivity 38
    The institutional model 39

3. The Domestic Model of Organization 47

   Unlimited time and energy 47
   Experience transmitted orally..................... 51
   Diffuse power relations 57
   Making room for children 63
   Space defines practice............................. 66
   Conclusion 72

4. Ideological Orientations of Various Types of
   Shelters... 77

   Service ideologies 80
   Four types of shelters 89

Conclusion... 107

Table 1 43
Table 2 98

Appendix 1: Guide to dealing with domestic
   violence 113

Appendix 2: List, by region, of women's shelters
   in Québec 115

Acknowledgements

I would like to thank especially Frédéric Lesemann, from the Université de Montréal; Nicole Kirouac and Danièle Fréchette, from the Regroupement provincial des maisons d'hébergement; Louise Forget, from the Escale pour Elle centre in Montréal; and Louise Vandelac, from the Université du Québec à Montréal, for their encouragement and assistance.

I would also like to thank the women in the centres for the inspiration they provided. I am grateful to the many people who assisted me at all stages of this study, although I cannot acknowledge them all by name.

Finally, I would like to thank Margaret Heap and Lorne Huston for their careful and sensitive translation of my book.

INTRODUCTION

What prompts a woman who has never had any direct experience with violence against women to take an interest in it? Perhaps to understand why we are afraid of violence, or to see what we can do about it. Women's shelters help us to do both.

The experience of women who are victims of violence is brutal testimony to a form of male domination that our society has taken pains to hide. Society is more willing to accept that a woman is sick, tired, depressed or overwhelmed by circumstances... It 'accepts' certain weaknesses in women and has developed very specialized services — administered mostly by men — to deal with them.

The very term 'battered women' is a recent addition to our vocabulary, barely a decade old. Women fought long and hard to have the problem recognized. Accepting this new perception requires that we overcome a social taboo that is still very much part of our culture.

We now know that the reason some women are fearful, mere shadows of their real selves, is that in their daily lives they are threatened, attacked and often physically injured. Although we are still in the process of discovering the full extent and ramifications of domestic violence, we are beginning to see that it is widespread.

Women do not want pills to wipe out the memories or bandaids to cover up the open wounds. They want to escape the violence and find support for their decision to seek justice. Women's shelters — or refuges, or transition houses — try to bring these needs into the open and respond to them.

This book will trace the development of women's shelters in Québec and examine the innovative nature of their work for society as a whole, as well as their contribution to the women's movement.

Shelters for women were an offshoot of the women's movement that since the early 1960s has been growing worldwide — in terms of both theoretical publications and pressure groups and social action. The first women's shelter was founded in Great Britain; from there the idea spread to the United States and throughout North America. Since 1976, women's houses in Québec have built a network of mutual aid that acts as a countervailing force to institutionalized relations between men and women.

In seeking help and support, the women whose plight is the most desperate — battered women — have thus chosen a familiar and anonymous battleground for combatting violence: the house, the home. They have reclaimed possession of the home and turned it into a place of action, and thus a public, political space. They have developed a support system so that women are no longer isolated in their attempts to break the vicious circle of violence. Working on the fringes of the institutional system of 'services,' they have founded shelters designed on a community model, created centres for collectively restoring their sense of self-worth and established a network for providing immediate, direct assistance. Rejecting the scientific models, they have chosen to work from women's experience.

This does not mean, however, that women's shelters have been exempt from the growing pains that inevitably accompany official recognition of such natural networks. Women's shelters seem to be autonomous but, in fact, they are subject to external influences — professional practices, government standards, scientific educational models. Can the two be reconciled? If the autonomous domestic model of organization is to hold its own against external influences and institutional models, it is urgent that we begin to reflect on the alternatives we would like to see.

The praxis of women's shelters in Québec can be fully understood only in the context of the ideology of the women's movement, with its many tendencies and components. The different ideologies of 'services' found among nuns, housewives and feminists have given rise to a whole range of shelters. But this typology is merely a pedagogical tool used to introduce the goals and methods of the shelters. The choices made relate to the material, historic and ideological conditions of women from all walks of life.

Women's shelters in Québec are a reflection of Québec society. Some are run by active feminists; others by socially committed nuns; yet others by ordinary wives and mothers who open their homes to other women. This book is not an attempt to describe an ideal movement. Rather, I wish to present real women who have decided to take action and work towards a common goal.

The reader will not find a scientific analysis. This book proposes a preliminary history and analysis that will be immediately accessible and useful to women's groups. The progress made during the first phase of the shelter movement must not be lost. I hope this book will encourage a self-awareness and re-appropriation of the experience of women's shelters.

This approach has its limitations, one of which may be that it favours one perception of women's shelters without giving sufficient consideration to alternative perceptions. And it is indeed true that since the thinking behind this book grows out of the women's movement and women's history, it tends to favour a certain definition of women's shelters. It is the shelter without words, the oral culture of women and the collective subconscious marked by women's wounds that I want to describe. Perhaps there is another model of women's shelters that is more 'professional,' a model for the future, reflecting a compromise between their operation and future needs. I can only hope that other studies will take up the debate and pursue the work begun here.

15

1

SHELTERS: A WOMEN'S STORY

Forgotten beginnings

In Québec, the 1960s brought the Quiet Revolution. The social unrest that was to peak in the 1970s fostered many different political, social and cultural organizations with a nationalist and socialist ideology.

Social and economic conditions resulted in a break with traditional values and the emergence of social protest movements. Reforms in state structures, health and education, along with the crisis in the family (a declining birth rate and a rising divorce rate), unionization of government employees, and secularization of Québec society, paved the way for progressive new ideas.

As more and more jobs opened up for educated women, they became increasingly conscious of their status as women. In 1968, English-speaking women organized the first consciousness-raising groups in Québec and American material on women's liberation began to circulate widely.

From 1969 to 1972, feminist struggles in Québec were for the most part the work of left-wing groups and centred on the abortion issue. The feminists of this period sought to fuse feminism, independence and socialism: a bold ambition, perhaps, but hardly utopian given the context at the time.

Tensions arising from the existence of various feminist tendencies in the same group led to splits and a profusion of pressure groups, all lobbying the government, but all fighting for sexual equality in their own way.

The three major tendencies were, and still are, the Marxist feminists, the radical feminists and the reformist feminists. Marxist feminists emphasize the relationship between class struggle and women's oppression. For radical feminists, the priority is the struggle against patriarchy. Reformist feminists seek primarily to improve the status of women without calling for radical change in the social structure.

All three tendencies were very active at all levels of society in the early 1970s, and often all three were involved in the same struggle. In rural areas, feminism was broadly based and largely reformist in nature. Radical feminism was more likely to develop in major urban centres.

In 1973, in response to lobbying by various groups, the provincial government created the Conseil du statut de la femme (CSF — Council on the Status of Women) for the promotion of women's rights. The first women's centres were founded the same year, notably the CIRF (Centre d'information et de référence pour femmes — Women's Information and Referral Centre, now the Women's Centre) in Montréal. These centres drew attention to the problem of battered women for the first time. The appeals for assistance, shelter and legal advice began to highlight a reality long buried by social taboos.

Perception of the existence of battered women as a social phenomenon rather than a series of individuals with individual problems contributed to the growth of a new solidarity among women. Without the women's movement and the lobbying and protest groups that nourished it, the problem of battered women would still be considered a private, individual problem, as it had been for centuries. But the militant women's groups were not afraid to confront violent men and the institutional complicity they traditionally enjoyed.

Women with relatively few resources at their disposal joined together to tackle a difficult job. They developed new approaches to a problem that had been written off by professional social workers as insoluble. Working in many cases without grants or subsidies, without recognition, without legal protection and without the aid of specialists, they began to expose a reality that had long been played down.

The history of battered women's shelters is a long chain of isolated efforts, day-to-day support and appeals for solidarity in all its forms. It is basically and fundamentally a history of women: the women who founded the shelters; the women who took a historic initiative when they decided to stop waiting for someone else to solve their problems; the women who proposed the first alternatives to the cycle of violence.

In the traditional professional approach to dealing with violence, the legal system and the police in effect aided and abetted the woman-beater. Moreover, medical and social services were powerless, in fact, to provide even short-term or intermediate solutions to the problem of spousal violence. Daily work with battered women underscored the lack of a safe place for them to go. A woman either was sent back home or went to stay with relatives. Whichever she chose, she remained vulnerable, easy to find, and thus a defenceless target for pressure and attack by her aggressor. The result was that she was forced to withdraw legal charges, resume her role as wife and mother and try to swallow her anger and bury her fear.

The women who founded and built women's shelters began by refusing to bury their heads in the sand any longer. It soon became apparent that their basic general approach was anti-professional. No battered woman would now be forced to go back home. The women working in the shelters would encourage the victims to tackle the real problem — violence in the home. They would ascertain how serious the problem was and begin to speak out about it. Battered women would not be separated from their children; their children would not be placed in foster homes or reception centres by social service authorities. Staff and volunteers would do their utmost to preserve and strengthen mother-child relationships. The shelters would no longer accept the official social service stance of powerlessness. They began to make maximum use of the scarce resources available and lobby for changes in legislation. They demanded copies of police and medical reports in order to compile statistics and case studies and thus come to grips with the scope of the problem.

In 1970, the federal Royal Commission on the Status of Women undertook to analyze the situation of women in all areas of social and economic life. It is a curious but telling fact that the Commission's report (known as the Bird Report) makes no mention of women who are victims of violence. Despite its sweeping and noble mandate, the Commission failed to grasp the dramatic situation in which many women were trapped. The Commission's 468 briefs, forty research reports and thousands of letters from women did not touch on the problem of battered women; this would only become a topic of public concern in the 1970s and 1980s. The Report's silence amounted to denying that physical abuse was in fact inflicted on certain women, or was a certain aspect of the status of women in general.

In its early days, the movement for battered women's shelters operated in near secrecy, with the participation of women from all walks of life and of every political hue: new feminists, left-wingers, middle-class volunteer workers, women in working-class neighbourhoods, religious and church workers, mothers, students. What drew them together was an awareness of the needs of women in difficulty, nothing more.

This semi-clandestine way of operating was basically strategy, a way of providing services without attracting too much attention. Independent women's groups and drop-in centres identified women's most obvious and pressing needs. These early groups were concerned with the isolation of housewives and their crying need for information about abortion, immigration law, legal rights and procedures.

The first shelters opened in 1975 in Montréal, Sherbrooke, Port-Alfred and Longueuil, partly at the initiative of the Association des familles monoparentales (Association of Single-Parent Families). The women who founded the shelters were generally well-educated and/or in secure economic circumstances. Some enjoyed institutional or government support.

By 1977-78, the number of shelters was increasing. Feminist shelters sponsored by women's information centres or independent women's groups were founded. Three more shelters opened in Montréal and another on the North Shore of the St. Lawrence River.

Another seven shelters were established in 1979 — one in Montréal and the rest in smaller towns or regional centres (Amos, Alma, Beauport, La Tuque, Gatineau and Hull). Various kinds of shelters and centres were added in 1980 and 1981, including three in Québec City and one each in Drummondville, Montréal, Sainte-Thérèse and Roberval. Since 1981, more have opened in the Gaspé péninsula, Rimouski and Saint-Hyacinthe. All in all, there are now between twenty-five and thirty shelters operating in Québec, with as many more in the planning stages. Stemming from a wide variety of backgrounds and influences, the shelters try to adapt to the specific environment in which they are located — neighbourhood, rural area, city or ethnic grouping.

So despite — or because of — the economic crisis, the last few years have brought many plans for centres and shelters in all parts of Québec. These more recent projects are linked to CLSCs, women's drop-in centres, independent women's groups, volunteer centres, and in some cases certain political structures (the local MP or MPP, for example).

In isolated regions, where the cost of a women's shelter and a team of workers is beyond the financial reach of individual villages and towns, a whole range of alternative solutions has developed. Networks have been established of women and families who can be contacted easily for advice and emergency help; they take immediate charge of women in danger and transfer them to regional shelters or women's centres the next day. Other new initiatives common to both big cities and isolated regions include setting aside a 'safe apartment' in housing co-ops.

Women organize in a network

The dozen or so shelters in the planning stages or operating in Québec in 1975-76 wanted to share information and work together for a certain cohesion and common understanding of the movement that both inspired their efforts and exceeded their capacities. Feeling their way along, the shelters sought to define a rallying point around which shelters could build the same solidarity that each of them extended to women in difficulty.

For this and other much more practical reasons, such as the many financial and organizational problems confronting the shelters, joint meetings became necessary. A department of the Conseil du statut de la femme (CSF), called Consult-Action, seemed to be the agency in the best position to help the shelters. Relatively new, the CSF was the only provincial government agency dealing with the status of women and was the most appropriate channel for contacting the government. As well, its stance was one of prudent, reformist feminism careful not to alienate any group of women by taking radical stands.

The appeal to the CSF took the form of repeated requests throughout 1976 for help and advice in maintaining or establishing centres for women in difficulty. The CSF acknowledged the importance of this issue and offered the shelters more or less temporary technical assistance. It proposed to publicize the problem of violence against women and delegate responsibility for this new social problem to the ministries concerned.

The first official meetings with the Ministry of Social Affairs took place in May 1978. The network of women's shelters remained an informal structure until February 1979, when it became the Regroupement provincial des maisons d'hébergement pour femmes en difficulté. This marked the end of secrecy and isolation for the shelters; a new period was beginning, in which their long-term but very real goal would be to achieve official recognition.

The Regroupement, or coalition, was actually very heterogeneous. The diversity of stated goals of the member groups was hard for some of them to accept, and for a few years this threatened to jeopardize all attempts at concerted action. All the tendencies in the women's movement were involved in this historic new endeavour, and a tremendous amount of work was required to hammer out common ground among them and build real solidarity, at least in terms of strategies for action.

Rural and urban groups differed on practically everything. There were ideological clashes and generation gaps over proposed solutions, with the younger, and in some ways more radical, women on one side and the more traditional women on the other. Pressure groups emerged and formed sub-groups to control the first organizational phase, which was characterized by strong institutional aspirations but little interest in autonomous action.

The new coalition finally succeeded in building a coherent network capable of playing a more active role in the future of the shelters. The tensions never outweighed the underlying tie that bound the shelters together, namely the experiences of women in difficulty and a common determination to help them.

All the shelters were in very precarious financial straits. Some of them were established as federal government Local Initiative Projects. Since LIP grants were a form of short-term aid intended to get unemployed people back into the labour market, they did not allow the shelters to hire people on any reasonably long-term basis. As a result, it was difficult to develop teams of well-qualified workers. The Conseil du statut de la femme turned to the provincial government for long-term funding specifically allocated for combatting violence against women.

Meanwhile, volunteer work continued to play a predominant role in running the shelters. This was in fact exactly what the government wanted: right from the start of negotiations with the Ministry of Social Affairs, the shelters came under the jurisdiction of the Service de soutien aux organismes bénévoles (volunteer work bureau).

The women were confronted with the dilemma of volunteer work. On the one hand, this allowed them to be relatively autonomous in their work; but on the other hand, it amounted to a way of merely perpetuating the current plight of women, namely economic dependence, and even poverty for some of them. Why should women always be volunteers? Should they be shouldering responsibility for an essential service, when it was really the state's job to provide it? It seemed they spent half their time and energy writing up briefs, reports, and applications for grants.

All they got in subsidies for 1977-78 was a pilot project of $100,000. It was not until 1980-81, after regional conferences on violence, that existing and planned shelters became eligible for regularly budgeted grants. These helped reduce the gap between the poorer and the better-funded shelters, although no clear policy on how grants were awarded was ever defined.

Financial survival was the primary reason for setting up the network of shelters. The internal structure and organization of the houses was a problem more easily addressed by each individual team of workers, but although some shelters originally hoped to solve their financial problems on their own, experience was to prove that collective struggles for an equitable solution for all the shelters was the better solution.

When the network was first set up, official social services were unaware, or at least acted as if they were unaware, of the problem of violence against women in the family. Social workers generally did not use the shelters. Gradually, a few Centres de services sociaux (CSS — social service centres) and a handful of doctors and lawyers began to refer women to the shelters. A very small number of professionals co-operated wholeheartedly, although these individuals were not representative of the institutions to which they were attached. It took the regional conferences on violence to make the professional world face up to the problem.

Logically or paradoxically, even the official services with family-oriented policies offered no kind of shelter or reception centre that protected the mother-child relationship. Any serious problem in the family or between spouses was liable to result in family break-up, with the children placed in foster families or institutions. Like all volunteer groups, the shelters provided a safety net for the victims of a problem that went unacknowledged or unresolved in the rigid structures of the big institutions.

A few CSSs took advantage of the valuable resource which the shelters constituted, providing them with some financial assistance and incorporating them into their emergency services. A dialectical interplay gradually developed between what the shelters had to offer and the battered women themselves, who began to express their needs more openly and more directly.

Co-operation with government services, so rare and provisional at first, was put on a more solid footing after the regional conferences on violence organized jointly by the Ministries of Justice and Social Affairs. The government now officially addressed the problem for the first time; and for the shelters it was the beginning of a working relationship with the state. The shelters had surfaced and achieved a certain public status. They remained private agencies, but their autonomy as yet meant very little.

The government takes charge

It was basically under the Parti québécois that the government began to move towards recognizing the shelters and according them some financial and organizational support. Preliminary work on the status of women was begun in 1973 with the creation of the Conseil du statut de la femme, but it is noteworthy that the first ministers with cabinet responsibility for the Conseil were not women.

The PQ formed the government in 1976. Social democracy, with the favourable prejudice it was presumed to have for women and women's issues, raised high hopes in the women's movement, and these hopes seemed confirmed a few years later when Lise Payette was appointed Minister for the Status of Women.

This was the context in which the movement for women's shelters evolved, influenced by similar developments in the United States and Europe. In terms of the women's movement, the network of women's shelters was basically service-oriented. And generally speaking, the women's movement in Québec has tended to provide services rather than build broad, radical, issue-oriented protest movements.

This reluctance to build broad common fronts stemmed undoubtedly from the fact that women are strongly conditioned towards the kind of work involved in providing services. Furthermore, the various groups had trouble agreeing on a common purpose and orientation in the struggles they undertook. In 1978, for example, an attempt to build a coalition against violence against women in Montréal failed to get off the ground, although this would have provided a very specific focal point for work with battered women. Generally, shelters were seen as a support and service rather than the nucleus of mass protest or broad pressure.

These service groups, with their strongly reformist tendencies, eventually managed to agree on certain key survival issues, such as the funding and general approach of the shelters. One of the shelters' key features was that their services were free: this was what made it possible for women to break out of the vicious circle of violence. This might seem to be a financial detail, but it was vital; if it was abandoned, things would go back to the way they used to be.

Furthermore, these groups were essentially based on practice rather than theory, and the sharing of that practice from shelter to shelter. A few feminist shelters considered that it was important to put time and energy into analyzing their work and its social and political consequences. Their theorizing dealt with the status of women, of course, but focussed more specifically on housework and the status of housewives, the material base for women's exploitation and oppression. After all, ninety per cent of the women who seek refuge within the shelters are housewives.

The organizational and ideological pluralism of the shelters constituted both their strong and their weak point in dealing with formal and one-dimensional government structures. Organizational difficulties were reflected in the shelters' precarious financial situation; in their extreme diversity which made it difficult to build coalitions; and ultimately in the way the PQ was able to co-opt women's struggles.

In 1980, at the demand of the Conseil du statut de la femme, the government took a number of steps to begin addressing the problem of violence against women. Its first initiative was a series of regional conferences on violence, which were the starting point for contacting professional circles and suggesting new ways of handling the problem. Following the conferences, subsidy programmes were developed. More than $1 million was budgeted for the continued existence of a number of houses, but others were frozen out without any clear explanation of the selection criteria used. There was an attempt to refuse all grants to those crisis centres dealing with sexual assault of any kind (CALACS — Centres d'aide et de lutte contre les agressions à caractère sexuel), reserving funding for the shelters coping with family violence. To all intents and purposes, this was an attempt to eradicate the groups fighting rape and to establish opposition between the two initiatives against violence.

The subsidies were soon accompanied by government measures to control the general approach of the shelters. The government instituted training courses for the personnel; proposed the use of forms similar to those used elsewhere in the social service network for compiling statistical data to identify the shelters' clientèle; and urged the shelters to put an end to their policy of free shelter.

As a result of all this subtle pressure, the coalition of shelters moved towards a policy of developing greater autonomy with regard to government intervention. The coalition wanted to preserve the progress it had made — for instance, the policy of allowing women to stay at the shelters free of charge; anonymity of the clients; and recognition of the anti-rape groups. The adoption of the principle of autonomy was interpreted by the coalition as a broad mandate making it the shelters' official intermediary with the Ministry of Social Affairs.

Nor was the question of subsidies ever really settled; it cropped up regularly every year, and many new projects were not receiving any subsidies at all.

Autonomy, which originally referred to the right of each centre or shelter to develop in its own way, took on a new meaning in light of government actions aimed at efficient, technocratic management and control. Much of the progress women had made in the struggle against violence now had to be protected against institutional solutions. The fact that it was often difficult to measure this progress in quantitative terms helped shield it from government yardsticks.

After all, you cannot measure women's political consciousness or the degree to which it has evolved. The new methods used by the shelters in their daily work created a domestic sphere that combined with the bureaucratic sphere and radically transformed it. The shelter evolved towards something that was neither quite a 'house' nor an 'institution,' but rather an alternative.

Taken as a whole, the shelters' attitude towards autonomy wavers between allegiance to the government and opposition to its policies. Consensus hammered out after long discussion seeks to reconcile the two tendencies in order to achieve a degree of self-management in the movement. State intervention has played an increasingly important role in the development of the network. Each new government policy is applied in a broader, more standard way, often totally ignoring the specific characteristics of the shelters.

But there is a question that remains to be answered: how can a movement that lies midway between daily life and politics continue to find its solutions in its own surroundings, in the solidarity of shelters and women, and in the fragile autonomy of shelters whose economic dependence makes them liable to public management and control?

Has the history of the shelters already reached the point where we must talk about giving the shelters back to women? Dispossession has always been an underlying danger in the history of the women's movement. Women must be especially lucid and vigilant to safeguard their original vision of the shelters and ensure that they develop at their own pace and on their own terms.

2

THE EMERGENCE OF WOMEN'S HOUSES

Choosing the battleground: the house

Why a house for women? After all, the house, the home, represents women's place and thus serves to reassure the society and the men who would preserve the status quo. The home isolates women, perpetuating the myth of domestic freedom and ensuring domestic productivity. Could women give the house another meaning? Could they make it into something beneficial to the thousands of women confronting the problem of social and family violence?

The very idea of a house for women embodies the principle of radical social change — going to a women's house, a shelter, means abandoning other houses. A women's house must be the very opposite of the home as defined by an economic system predicated on the social division of work that keeps women trapped in the home.

A women's house is an alternative to solitude, a first step towards refusing women's historic lot, a liberating response to the confinement peculiar to women who are victims of violence.

These women's houses raise two questions: what do they signify to the women who take shelter in them? and what meaning did their founders seek to give them?

An alternative to loneliness

Erin Pizzey, the woman who founded the first shelter for women in England in 1971, noticed that the women she met at demonstrations against rising prices were lonely and unable to do anything about it.

> As we stood on the street corners, we met lots of young mothers who all complained about the same thing — isolation. They felt cut off in their homes. This is really what set Women's Aid in motion...[1]

The solitude of women in the home had already been discussed in numerous studies of the condition of women, and it would be further extensively analyzed, in an attempt to come to grips with the essential aspects of the problem.

Germaine Greer associated this isolation with the housewife's lack of a 'social existence':

> The home is her province, and she is lonely there. She wants her family to spend time with her for her only significance is in relation to that almost fictitious group.[2]

Marilyn French has emphasized how harmful this loneliness can be, driving some women to madness:

> ...the outside world is hostile to them. They sit in silent kitchens, simmering, wondering if they are insane, knowing they are alone.[3]

According to Betty Friedan, the fundamental human dimension threatened by this solitude is a woman's identity:

> She does not know who she is herself. She waits all day for her husband to come home at night to make her feel alive.[4]

Lack of social existence; madness; loss of identity: three dimensions of the solitude that is a direct consequence of the economic system.

This is why women's houses must be communities, places "where women and their children could come to meet and escape, for a time, from loneliness."[5] The solidarity offered by a small women's house can be the first breach in this solitude.

Rejecting the house as a symbol of women's duty

Circumstances soon transformed Québec information and drop-in centres into shelters for battered women and transition houses for women in particular difficulty. Many houses hid their identity and 'went underground' in order to ensure the safety of the women and children who took shelter in them.

At first — and even today — these houses were sometimes labelled 'deviant' because their very existence set off changes in social relationships between men and women. The shelters have in effect given hundreds of women 'permission to leave home,' in contrast to the traditional institutions that were powerless to do anything except send women back home.

Angry husbands seized on this 'deviance,' but there was political reaction as well. For instance, a provincial cabinet minister in British Colombia was of the opinion that

> If we begin to establish transition houses, it's as if we wanted to sytematically separate families.[6]

Such reactions serve to remind us that the dominant ideology gives short shrift to any view of the family which strays from the model consecrated and perpetuated by the existing economic system.

This explains why many of the women who founded the houses were dismissed as 'abnormal'; they created places perceived as veritable centres of domestic guerilla warfare, threatening the existing economic and social order. The transformation of these houses into branch offices of social service agencies is a striking example of how society co-opts and neutralizes ideas that are too innovative for the social and economic climate from which they emerge. It can be expected that in coming years conservative forces in society will propose ways of further reducing this concept to an acceptable mould.

Permitting women to leave home means, in part, permitting them to abandon their assigned social role without necessarily resorting to a stay in hospital (an escape mechanism encouraged by society). In the past, a few days in hospital was all many battered women had to heal their wounds. A hospital stay was merely another routine phase in the cycle of violence.

For those who refused to admit, even to themselves, the collective issues at stake, the action of the women who founded the houses and those who took shelter in them could only be explained as abnormal behaviour. As Alberto Melucci has explained:

> When domination becomes a way of life, opposition to it necessarily seems marginal and deviant.[7]

This means that

> Advanced societies have more and more agencies for 'treating' social needs and demands that are potentially conflictual.[8]

Women's houses could become this kind of agency if their activities are determined solely by government standards or the professional norms prevailing in institutions. However, since women's houses grew out of the women's movement, they necessarily challenge a social system that is oppressive for women, and particularly battered women.

For an isolated woman, the freedom to leave home is like a worker being able to strike. The boss says, "Come back to work and then we'll negotiate." The husband-boss demands the same: first come back home. If no agreement is reached, the conflict goes to arbitration, or marriage counselling in domestic conflicts. This is often a pretence to get the woman to go back home without any change whatsoever in the fundamental contract.

Seen in this light, marriage counselling is not the neutral psychological tool it claims to be. If carried out in a sexist way, it is an integral part of the dominant-dominated relations between men and women.

But why would women use an instrument as simple and commonplace as a house to wage this struggle? Why would women paradoxically seek to combat the violence carried out in the privacy of the home with a system of defence based primarily on houses? Because when all of society's structures proved powerless to deal with the problem of conjugal violence, women chose the battleground they knew best, and then transformed it.

A women's house sits in the midst of other houses, anonymous behind its fragile doors and windows that look like any other doors and windows — the weapon of a domestic and feminine guerilla. The symbol of women's duty has become the symbol of their revolt and refusal; their domestic jail has become their first step towards liberation.

For the liberation of a women's house

A women's house is the unexpected answer to

> The isolation which makes the red-brick-villa household so neurotic... the intense introverted anguish of the single eye-to-eye confrontation of the isolated spouses....[9]

It offers an escape from the home that is a trap for some, a gilded cage for others, laying bare the sterility and lack of freedom in many women's lives, regardless of their economic and social standing. Is violence the exception, or is it the direct result of a social structure "which recognizes the sexist, economic and ideological oppression of women, both inside and outside the home"?[10]

If a system requires that women remain isolated in their homes and puts male waged workers in charge, it is to be expected that some situations will inevitably deteriorate into violence.

It is always revealing to ask a battered woman how her spouse acts during periods of crisis. He usually tries to instill fear in his victim and make her feel cut off and trapped inside the home. The woman is left with no alternatives, sometimes not even any relatives. She doesn't know where to go if she dares venture beyond the prison wall drawn around her; and if she does dare to transgress the boundary mentally or physically, she is liable to be pursued, spied upon, threatened and brought back inside. In extreme cases, she is threatened with injury or death if she seeks freedom.

Lenore Walker, who has used the work of Martin Seligman to demonstrate how battered women *learn* to become 'victims' in successive crisis situations with their spouses, argues that once victims realize that they can do something about their situation, they lose at least some of their sense of helplessness:

> However, once they did learn that they could make the voluntary response, their helplessness disappeared.[11]

For those who succeed in breaking out of the trap, a women's house represents an alternative, 'somewhere else.' Leaving home is a first step towards controlling one's situation.

The next steps — seeking recourse, exercising one's rights, rejecting the role of victim — stem from the first:

> As soon as battered women walk through the door, they are no longer helpless victims.[12]

In this sense, the houses are schools for liberation, and with their help some women can reach their potential. Others go part way and then stop, accomplishing only one step with each stay. The means put at their disposal are the same in both cases, however. A woman who goes back to her spouse after modifying the contract between herself and her husband, or after having learned something about her legal position and her rights, is not exactly the same woman in exactly the same circumstances as before. She knows where to go when the next crisis happens; she is no longer really alone.

The houses as they were founded

What did the women who founded and ran these houses want them to be? Three aspects were considered very important: it was vital that the houses be women's houses first and foremost; that they constitute a response to a new need; and that they provide a forum for politicizing a problem previously judged to be private.

A women's house

At Chiswick Women's Aid, the most radical expression of the women's house concept, the house belongs to all the women. Any woman who wants a key can have one. Men are admitted by invitation only. This basic and very clear distinction is already an assertion of the principle of 'self-help': women must rely primarily on themselves, on their solidarity as women and their capacity for mutual aid.

This principle contradicts the social ideology that women should rely on men, particularly within the institution of marriage, holding that a man can and should be a woman's provider, defender and protector.

Society has always implied that a group of women would have trouble surviving on their own. Women who have joined together to successfully accomplish major projects are rare; women see themselves as isolated.

In contrast, we are used to seeing men do business together, engage in politics together, wage war together, and meet in their private clubs.

The only places women have in which to meet are their houses, and the idea of a women's house involves something very new. Here, women start studying the laws and social policies that oppress them. They begin to see the links between their personal problems, and they begin to organize for broad social action.

An emerging response to a real need

A women's house is basically a response to a problem for which society had failed to find a solution. This approach avoided the danger of outside agents being parachuted in with methods and goals foreign to the problem.

A women's house strives to be all-encompassing, providing both a living environment and a setting for consciousness-raising and action. It is thus autonomous and relatively marginal in relation to its social surroundings.

According to Lenore Walker, Chiswick Women's Aid was founded on the "total therapeutic community model."[13] Each woman is responsible for her own well-being and that of the others. Decisions are reached by consensus. The women have confidence that other women will help them and that they themselves are capable of giving satisfactory help to others. This is the foundation for the slow process of accepting responsibility for one's own life and for the lives of others.

A women's house transforms the 'house' into a centre for learning one's rights and the cornerstone of a general approach which serves as both a community and a domestic model. In the next chapter we will examine the various implications of this domestic model.

The house as a public forum

The women who founded the first women's houses did not seek to merely transpose domestic dramas from one house to another without any public action around this exodus of women from their homes. Erin Pizzey has published a steady stream of articles in both British and foreign newspapers about the plight of these women and the network of help and support for them that now extends far beyond the borders of Great Britain.

In Québec, the movement for women's houses has been accompanied by research and publications. At the request of the houses and shelters, documents on the subject prepared by the Conseil du statut de la femme (CSF) have been widely distributed. The slogan chosen was "To start with, let's talk about it..."[14]

As well, each house seeks newspaper coverage, partly to publicize its existence as a resource for women and partly to publicly condemn violence against women by telling about women's encounters with the legal and social service systems. Many of the case histories stem from women's experiences with authorities while staying at the shelters; and others come to light when women feel free to open up about previous experiences in the safety of a women's house. This growing bank of oral histories adds to our understanding of the violence against women and its consequences.

Over the years, these personal histories have coalesced into an oral tradition that has become the basic reference point for understanding the problem of battered women.

Women's individual histories intersect for a time with the history of the houses. Their life stories continue outside the houses, too, of course, although perhaps in anonymity. Many women, however, return periodically to the houses to take stock of their situation and thus remain visible for a number of years, adding to the bank of oral testimony.

Women have made a public issue of violence behind the closed doors of the home, and they have done it in their own way — through social analysis backed up by hundreds of case histories.

Taking the issue to the public has served to inform both the public and institutional personnel and to make it into a social issue for which citizens and the government must take shared responsibility:

> With the links that are growing between groups in all these countries we will have a large platform of radical opinion from which to change official policy.[15]

Thus the purpose of a women's house is diametrically opposed to the secret home that stifles the cries and hides the tensions from even the closest neighbours. Seeking to make public a domain that has until now been considered private is a political act; it bothers people.

Now that shelters for battered women exist, it has become obvious that violence against women is not an exceptional phenomenon. It could not occur as consistently and as frequently as it does if it were not an integral part of the power structures that govern Western society, supposedly the most liberal in the world.

Institutional counter-productivity

Right from the beginning, women realized that they could not copy institutional models. The institutions had failed; in fact, by advising women to go back home they were officially perpetuating institutional counter-productivity:

> ...it has now become obvious that if the undesirable side-effects of most institutions are taken into account, institutions no longer

look like instruments of progress; instead, they appear to be the main obstacles to achieving the very goals that are their avowed purpose.[16]

Battered women were provided with services, but not the safety which they needed. Social workers did not explain their rights to them, and did not help them defend and exercise those rights.

Erin Pizzey tells how some social service agencies simply put families into taxis and paid their fare to Chiswick.[17] And Lorraine Godard, while working at the Centre de la femme nouvelle, told a conference in 1978 that while most of the needs of a battered woman could 'theoretically' be met by existing social services, in practice they were not. This is still true today:

> A high proportion of women referred to the Centre de la femme nouvelle were referred by social service agencies and/or their therapist. Was this a tacit recognition of the inadequacy of their kind of therapy (non-feminist... inasmuch as a feminist orientation entails a social vision of the situation of women)?[18]

Godard went on to examine the influence of the social standards assimilated by battered women and the orientation of the services offered.

The institutional model

What most troubled the founders of women's houses about the way institutions dealt with battered women were lack of any sense of urgency in crisis situations; lack of any immediate assistance to provide shelter for a family in distress; and ignorance of how serious and dangerous the situation could be for these women.

Imagining what a women's house can be means seeing a different model of the family and different relations between men and women and between women and other women. It is at this ideological level that official institutions have displayed the least creativity.

Although the professionals who staff the institutions are familiar with marriage and family breakdown, and although a certain liberalization in attitudes has paved the way for new and innovative services to the public, the techniques at the disposal of the professionals nonetheless still tend to be oriented towards the traditional extended 'family.'

Comments from a few social workers currently dealing directly with instances of violence would seem to indicate that in many ways their situation resembles that of the victims of violence:

— they are threatened, in some cases sufficiently to instill a permanent sense of fear;

— they realize that they are neither protected nor backed up with team support by the agencies for which they work;

— if they try to discuss their dangerous experiences with colleagues, they are soon singled out as incompetent. They are told they did not intervene skillfully or diplomatically enough, or did not try the right technique... They are frequently asked, "What have you done for the couple?" and have no choice but to admit, "I haven't done anything for the couple";

— isolated in official agencies where it is difficult for professionals to keep their work anonymous, the social workers' experiences are similar to those of their clients; they know from daily experience that violence exists but that it is ignored by society and social work agencies.

In these circumstances, many social workers are forced to open a file, take whatever professional action they are supposed to take and then quickly close the file or transfer the case.

The greatest merit of the women's houses in all this has been that they foster conditions that prevent co-optation and that make it possible to intervene directly in violent situations. The fact that the houses are anonymous (especially in urban areas) prevents the aggressor from interfering with their work, while support from the staff ensures that neither the victim nor the woman working with her suffer from isolation. This builds trust and helps them overcome their fear, particularly in the face of serious threats.

It is therefore hardly surprising that development of the houses entailed rejection of the institutional model, with its professionalism and its bureaucracy. This reaction is characteristic of all movements that challenge the institutional order.

The women's houses do not escape the major dilemma currently facing the women's movement: should the emphasis be put on equality or on the differences between men and women? Depending on which aspect of the social problem is being considered, the strategy will sometimes focus on equality, other times on the differences.[19]

In many of their choices — concerning issues, techniques, structures — women's houses have chosen to emphasize a dimension that is important to women: the domestic model. The women who take shelter in the houses are all familiar with this model — for many of them, it is the only one they know. The women who work there are also confronted with the domestic model on a daily basis and cannot perceive it as a neutral element in their organization.

In choosing not to reject the domestic model, preferring instead to incorporate it into the general structure of the house, the women renewed the tradition of a feminist school dating back to the early twentieth century. The 'material feminists' (c. 1880-1920) sought to revolutionize the material condition of women; and, unlike Engels and Lenin, they saw value in domestic work, refusing to accept the idea that equality depends on a women's ability to replace men in the office or factory.[20]

Louise Vandelac refers to the material feminist school in discussing the model of autonomous and domestic organization:

> The traditional gap between liberated-waged-working women and alienated housewives must be questioned. Our demands and struggles are still modelled too closely on those of the labour movement. Women's groups have developed on a domestic organizational model in which time and energy are not quantified, lessons are transmitted through oral tradition, and power relations are diffuse. These groups must confront institutions operating on a totally different basis. Consequently, the balance of power between them is never equal.

> One of the challenges of the women's movement is precisely that of preserving the positive aspects that have enabled it to develop an autonomous model of organization while beginning to think out the kinds of demands and alternatives it wants to promote.[21]

Acknowledgement of the differences, and control over them, is a basic prerequisite for equality. The domestic model has been abandoned in recent feminist struggles because it had been devalued. It was defined by men as unimportant and relegated to the sphere of private life. Women's houses have accepted the challenge of working with this organizational model and making it into a collective, communal and subversive model. They realize subconsciously that:

> It is at the daily, anthropological level that women are strong. It is at the level of the multiple powers they are constantly challenging that women are a formidable political force in society today.[22]

Women's houses have thus taken daily experience as the starting point for their work, using the domestic model. To analyze this model, we will use Louise Vandelac's themes:

— time and energy are not quantified;
— experience and progress are transmitted orally;
— power relations are diffuse.

We will add two other themes that in our opinion are important to understanding the value and depth of the domestic model:

— the role of children;
— domestic space.

Referring to Table 1 will make it easier to understand these themes and their evolution in the houses.

Table 1

	PHASE 1 FOUNDING	PHASE 2 PAID STAFF	PHASE 3 UNIONIZATION
VERSATILITY	almost complete	tasks increasingly defined	– tasks defined by contract – divided into manual and intellectual tasks
RIGHTS	absent	subject of concern and discussion	guaranteed by collective agreement
DISTANCING	egalitarian relations	begins to develop	relations – employer/workers – residents/staff become more rigid
ORGANIZATION	informal	gradually becomes more formal	relations may be perceived as hierarchical and oppressive

Notes

1. Erin Pizzey, *Scream Quietly or the Neighbours Will Hear.* Harmondsworth, England: Penguin Books, 1974, p. 9.
2. Germaine Greer, *The Female Eunuch.* New York: Bantam Books, 1972, p. 239.
3. Marilyn French, *The Bleeding Heart.* New York: Summit Books, 1980, p. 258.
4. Betty Friedan, *The Feminine Mystique.* New York: Dell, 1977, p. 24.
5. Erin Pizzey, *op. cit.*, p. 9.
6. Transition House, *A Study of Battered Women,* Vancouver, 1976.
7. Alberto Melucci, "Société en changement et nouveaux mouvements sociaux," *Sociologie et sociétés,* Vol. 10, No. 2 (1978), p. 49.
8. *Ibid.*
9. Germaine Greer, *op. cit.*, p. 234.
10. Maurice Moreau, "A structural approach to social work practice," *Canadian Journal of Social Work Education,* Vol. 5, No. 1 (1979), p. 83.
11. Lenore Walker, *The Battered Woman.* New York: Harper and Row, 1979, p. 46.
12. *Ibid.*, p. 198.
13. *Ibid.*, pp. 193-194.
14. Marie Leclerc, *Pour commencer, parlons-en...* CSF, Québec Government, 1978.
15. Erin Pizzey, *op. cit.*, p. 137.
16. Ivan Illich, *Némésis médicale.* Paris: Seuil, 1975. Illich's book has also appeared in English (*Medical Nemesis: The Expropriation of Health.* London: Calder and Boyars, 1975), but this passage is not found as such in the English version.
17. Erin Pizzey, *op. cit.*, p. 30.
18. Lorraine Godard, "Femmes battues," a lecture given to nursing students at the Université de Montréal, 1978.

19. The dilemma here goes beyond the question of emphasizing equality or difference. The basic dilemma concerns the production/reproduction of women. On this, see Louise Vandelac's article in *Sociologie et sociétés,* Vol. 13, No. 2 (October 1981), pp. 67-82.
20. Dolores Hayden, *The Grand Domestic Revolution.* Cambridge, Mass.: MIT Press, 1981, p. 3.
21. Gisèle Bourret, "Autour du 8 mars: propos de Louise Vandelac," *Presse-Libre,* March 1981.
22. Yolande Cohen, "Réflexions désordonnant les femmes du pouvoir," in *Femmes et politique,* Le Jour, 1981, p. 217. A shorter English version of this article appears in Angela Miles and Geraldine Finn, eds., *Feminism in Canada: From Pressure to Politics.* Montréal: Black Rose Books, 1982.

3

THE DOMESTIC MODEL OF ORGANIZATION

Unlimited time and energy

If we look at the immense variety of work involved in running a women's house — from taking care of babies to social work — it is obvious that the range of tasks requires versatility and multiple skills. It is also obvious that it is all too easy to devote endless time and energy to the work.

The principle of 'self-help' encourages women to take action on all fronts at once, despite the limited number of staff and volunteers. To take just one example, the houses make use of the media without resorting to specialists in public relations, yet both the French and English-language media are contacted regularly every year on the issue of battered women. Some health professionals and social workers consider that autonomous women's groups rely too much on 'self-help' and are in danger of 'burnout.'

In the early stages, in particular, the houses were run rather recklessly. Unfamiliar with the basic principles and dynamics of helping relationships, the staff invested totally in their relations with the women they sought to help, becoming very emotionally involved in the process. In their ignorance of the legal and police systems they got involved in cases where even the police had no legal right to intervene. As a result, some women quite unwittingly found themselves caught up in situations that bore more resemblance to American gangster films than to any imaginable kind of social work.

Despite the excesses, however, their determination to support battered women produced some interesting results. To start with, the problem was defined very clearly. Women were horrified to discover that society offered no protection to the battered woman.[1]

Three stages can be distinguished in the way time and energy was invested in women's houses in Québec. Put very simply, the volunteers of the first phase eventually became paid employees, and later unionized employees.

In the first, volunteer phase, very few of the women who worked in the houses were paid to do so, and they received little co-operation, or even a willingness to co-operate, from the established institutions. These early volunteers worked as if everything depended on their own personal commitment. Women spent sixty-hour shifts in the shelters; in some houses the staff lived in, sharing their entire lives with the women taking refuge. The result was that there was very little 'distance' between the staff and the residents. It was a period of great idealism — there was so much to be done, and the women were determined to do it all. There was a great sense of urgency about everything the houses undertook.

With time, however, new perceptions led to a marked change in attitude among the indefatigable volunteers. The women who staffed the houses began to realize that improvements in the situation of the most vulnerable women, the victims of violence, were achieved at the expense of their own working conditions. Paradoxically, the more efficient and effective the houses were, the less likely it was that society would ever do anything about the problem.

This realization paved the way for the second phase. A few of the volunteers were hired as regular staff. They bacame the core of a team of paid workers that characterized each house. The teams had to make choices about personnel and salaries. Generally speaking, they either opted for an egalitarian, socializing model or else chose the pattern of the existing collective agreements in the social affairs network.[2] The houses began to conform to certain basic working conditions — the right to be paid for one's work, the right to a reasonable schedule of work, the right to annual vacations, training, etc.

The emotional overload that is the rule in these houses meant that the staff needed special provisions for time off, and some of the houses did provide this.[3] As well, a growing awareness of all aspects of the problem of battered women and increased familiarity with the professional guidelines of other social workers made the women working in the houses more self-assured and effective in their work.

Versatility is a necessity in running a home. Look at what mothers must know how to do, for instance. They must be teachers for their children, psychologists for their husbands and generally in charge of personal relations in the home. They must manage the family budget, ensure reproduction, and are responsible for the kitchen and housekeeping. All of this is equally true in the women's houses.

In the second phase, however, this generalized versatility has been put into question. There is no longer an attempt to have the entire team working simultaneously with all the women in the shelter. Follow-up is done in a more organized way and specialized tasks develop. Three major job areas emerge — administration, group life and counselling, and support work.

In the initial phase, it was not uncommon to see a co-ordinator who had just finished the grocery shopping interviewing a new arrival at the shelter before sitting down to write a grant application. But in the second stage, this kind of 'Jill-of-all-trades' was by-and-large phased out. Today, the co-ordinators co-ordinate and manage. Their involvement in group activities and counselling is limited to discussion at meetings and very circumscribed, semi-professional tasks.

The job area that remains most closely related to domestic organization is group life and counselling, which involves internal management of the house. This preliminary specialization was the intermediate step bridging the 'Jill-of-all-trades' model and an organizational model in which there is a division of labour between manual and intellectual tasks. While the latter theoretically allows all the women to participate in the work and the ideological orientation of the group, in practice power struggles lead to hierarchy.

The houses do not all follow the pattern of development described in Table 1. Any typology inevitably involves a simplification of real situations. Some houses — the exceptions to the rule — were run at a level of centralization and specialization approaching that of institutions right from the start. This was a choice these houses made in setting their original goals and they had the professional and financial resources required to operate in such a manner.

Generally speaking, though, the circumstances under which the shelters were founded meant opting for makeshift solutions. These houses now operate with paid staff. Some are trying to reconcile the goals they set when they were founded with the means at their disposal now that workers are paid.

The newest houses incorporate some aspects of the 'paid-staff' phase but are still characterized by the spirit of the founding phase in terms of their approach and working conditions.

At the present time, there is only one house in Québec that is unionized, for reasons peculiar to the history of that house. The most plausible explanation is that the regular staff in this house never had the opportunity to gradually acquire the rights associated with the 'paid-staff' phase. Unionization was seen as a way for the workers to win recognition of their rights.

Although this is the only house that has been organized so far, unions are definitely in the offing for other houses. The CSN[4] has already begun an organizing drive in the provincial network. Unionization is still largely a male-dominated process that raises many unsettled questions for women; for example, whether the collective is an alternative to unionization for a feminist group. Without choosing to be a collective, many houses prefer a system of communication that is more flexible and less hierarchical than the union model, and are loathe to codify every last detail of the organization of work. Given the limited number of workers in each house, it will be interesting to see how long they will be able to preserve the spontaneous daily working relations that make the domestic model so flexible.

This choice is seriously testing the determination of the shelter movement to preserve its autonomy. Society's failure to offer solutions leaves staff in the women's houses in a dilemma: while working all-out on behalf of the most disadvantaged women, they must at the same time strive to avoid

> reproducing female ghettos by creating the kind of job that reinforces the sector of activity traditionally reserved for women.[5]

These two goals are likely to remain contradictory and mutually harmful unless ways of reconciling them are found that allow one struggle to sustain and even serve as a model for the other.

This dilemma also highlights the ambivalence of the domestic organizational model if it is not seen as autonomous. In houses where this model merely serves to reinforce women's oppression and create substandard jobs for them, it will not play the subversive role that could make it a real alternative. Semi-institutional solutions threaten to turn the houses into empty shells where all the innovative features of the domestic model cannot be fully exploited as alternatives to the institutional model.

Experience transmitted orally

The women's movement has led to a certain number of realizations. Women know beyond a shadow of a doubt that they do not have a voice in society. The corollary is that what women say is worthless.

> Women's lack of power in our culture is reflected in their language...an emotional language...[6]

One result of the women's movement was that women created places where they could talk and where their words counted. Women's comments, previously confined to private life and dismissed as chatter, became an organized and organizing force.

Women's houses are one of these forums where women's words have been redefined and given new dimensions. What makes these forums different is that they are for victims. The language of victims is precious; at times it is little more than an inarticulate cry as they emerge from a desert.

Sorrow, hope, guilt, fear: the victims can voice their experiences, their lives, without thinking they are mad, without doubting themselves. Their words are heard and understood. Then, as emotional language meets with the more rational language of rights, action and information, it is structured and reoriented.

The institutional model favours technical and bureaucratic language. The professional works with files. Much time and energy is spent writing technical messages. There is no collective voice; discussions take place between individual clients and social workers. In such a system, power lies in the control of important files.

Affirming that lessons and experience are transmitted orally in the domestic organizational model means emphasizing these two dimensions:

— women must speak out on the basis of their daily lives;

— our relation to the written word must be examined with a view to restoring the relation between those who write and those who are written about; this raises the whole question of written files.

Authentic and autonomous words

There is no question that women's houses have created an autonomous discourse, a discourse not previously held by any professional or official circles. They have developed a new perception of a social need and the corresponding social action. Yet, paradoxically, although practices in the houses are evolving fairly rapidly, the discourse has remained much the same.

As is the case with all analyses, heavy use is made of this discourse to get across a message and influence people's way of thinking. It is not free of contradictions, but it has the great advantage of being related to real life, and adapts continually to the ebb and flow of real life. For instance, most of the newspaper reports, videos, films and books on social issues produced by women's houses have been directly inspired by the behaviour and experiences of battered women. Cristina Perincioli, who founded the West Berlin Women's Help Centre in 1976, has directed a film whose title translates as *Women's Patience is Men's Strength*, scripted directly from the women's own accounts and in which the women play themselves.[7]

The spoken word outweighs the written, just as it does in the private home. Personal interaction is very important. As soon as a woman arrives at a women's house, she is offered an opportunity to join group discussions. She can listen to other women talk about their experiences and tell her own story. She is also caught up right from the start in a language of action: what have the other women done to begin solving their problems? What will she do to solve hers?

She learns that her secret problem, known only to her husband and perhaps a few relatives, is not really a personal secret at all: she shares the same problem with other women and she can find ways of helping women who are still isolated. Emotional language helps overcome a woman's isolation and transforms the emotions characteristic of victims — fear, guilt, powerlessness — into the emotions of action — strength, confidence, anger.

In the domestic model of organization, however, there is a danger that the discourse will wear thin and focus too narrowly on women's individual problems, at the expense of a social analysis of these problems. There is also the risk of falling into the clichés that traditionally characterize the conditioning of all women. Some of the houses organized along more traditional lines have fallen into this trap. It is therefore important to strive constantly to add new dimensions to the domestic model. This is what makes it subversive:

> Even though the authentic voice of women is profoundly subversive
> of the current social order, we can hope that as we articulate and

communicate it, more and more women will recognize it as their own.[8]

Women seeking refuge are defined in men's words: even after they leave their homes, they remain prisoners of this discourse that conditions their entire behaviour. The threats and scorn are walls that effectively isolate them from one another. And the male discourse comes back into play as soon as they establish contact, even through the intermediary of a lawyer.

A woman's experience in a women's house is therefore primordial. It is very important for her to try to analyze and reject a discourse that denies her individual existence, defines her as someone else's property and confines her within narrowly defined limits, even depriving her of contact with relatives. In doing so, a woman often gains her first perception of herself after months or years of non-existence.

One of the most effective practices in women's shelters is the mutual sharing of personal experiences by residents and staff. These conversations do not occur in the bureaucratic context of appointments, offices, professional distance and rationed time. They happen in the atmosphere of an extended family, the only effective way of reaching many women. Easy access to resources is another characteristic of the domestic model so familiar to all women.

These discussions also have very specific purposes, such as:

— proposing alternative lifestyles for women;

— making feminist analysis accessible as a daily part of all aspects of life in the houses;

— giving the women's movement the broad grounding it lacked at the turn of the century. Women from all walks of life can free themselves from their conditioning and try to redefine themselves. All they have to do is create places where they can collectively value themselves as women.

Relating to the written word

Erin Pizzey established a way of relating to the written word at Women's Aid that turned the traditional client/professional, helped/helper relationship upside-down. Her basic principle was quite simple:

the women seeking shelter were given control of the open diary, or log book, mail, and information in general:

> No one but the mothers taking refuge in the house may answer the telephone or sit behind the small desk and run the open diary.[9]

Control of the written word both confers and reflects power, a fact that did not escape the notice of the women who founded the first shelters. Women who are victims are powerless; withholding information from them would be to continue depriving them of power. It would make them 'clients' of social services. This is why Erin Pizzey justified her choices with an analysis of power:

> ...it is a safeguard to stop well-meaning do-gooders from coming in and taking over the source of power and information. The diary records all the daily happenings at Women's Aid and the cases who phone in. For a new mother who has been down-trodden and systematically destroyed for years, the fact that she is required to run the office gives her back a belief in her own ability and worth.[10]

All the shelters have basically copied this model, although only a few houses self-managed by women's collectives have applied it in radical form. At Ishtar Women's Resource Centre and Transition House, for instance, the concern for reducing paperwork to a minimum means that files are nothing more than a single contact sheet:

> Women are encouraged to fill out sections of the Contact Sheet themselves so that they have control over the information which is presented.[11]

At the Maison des femmes de la Côte-Nord in Baie-Comeau, Québec, residents are invited to write in the log book. Other houses seem to agree that 'real records' should not be kept. Women have access to information in a different way that does not seem to create problems.

55

As well, each house keeps a notebook or log in which calls for help and events in the house are recorded.

Gradually, however, information winds up in the hands of the staff. Residents have easy access to it, but not direct control. Some houses have two notice boards, one for staff and another for residents. Others have separate information offices for staff and residents. A number of houses leave residents temporarily in charge at night, during staff meetings, and so on.

The fact that the houses are small means that information can circulate fairly spontaneously and communally. Events in the media, news about residents and former residents, what is going on in the group: all is food for discussion. It certainly seems that 'small is beautiful.'

Experiences are passed on verbally, reducing the written word to a minimum. In the early stages, records, memos, minutes of meetings, etc. were either cheerfully ignored or kept to a bare minimum. Erin Pizzey remarked somewhat irreverently:

> House meetings are held every week, but so far we have never had to hold a committee meeting and pass out minutes and agendas, and I hope we never shall.[12]

But they did, or at least others did; and by 1982 houses in Québec were characterized by lots of meetings and lots of written documents of greater or lesser importance. Relations with the provincial Ministry of Social Affairs and government institutions mean that things have to be written down. Messages and experiences are still passed on orally within the houses, but written communications are now the rule in relations with the outside. Any house that refused to communicate in writing would be depriving itself of important contacts. It would relegate itself to a marginal role and in the long run cut itself off from subsidies.

Within the houses, the relationship with the written word is also changing. Women have several possibilities. What should they do? Write reports on children's behaviour and work with the Director of Youth Protection and other agencies? Emphasize conjugal problems and keep 'real records'? Or continue to assert the fundamental truth in the alternative that gave rise to the houses, namely that what counts is what women say day-to-day.

Diffuse power relations

In the domestic model of organization, power relations are diffuse. Family activities themselves are the organizing principle around which everything else is structured. There is often a strong taboo against *visible* power structures in the family group, for society has an interest in obfuscating these structures, and individuals tend to accept the cover-up as valid.

In general, society recognizes the man as head of the family, with all the privileges conferred by social institutions. Women only recently ceased to be minors in the eyes of the law. They have acquired the right to vote and to have political opinions that differ from those of their husbands. A woman can now keep her own name and shares in the right to dispose of the family residence. Power structures in the modern family have been identified and exposed by feminist analysis and struggle.

In groups like women's houses that have had to hammer out agreement on specific goals, the visibility of power structures was a problem right from the beginning. The various solutions that have been tried can be divided into two kinds: semi-institutional and anarchic.

The semi-institutional solution

A number of houses have adopted a semi-institutional model of organization for their internal management. In this model, information and decisions are communicated along hierarchical lines. The group does not talk about equality in managing the house, and this reflects a lack of any such equality in practice.

In the semi-institutional model, the co-ordinator is the 'manager.' This entails certain privileges — for example, exclusive use of a desk or room as an office. The manager makes the decisions and looks after relations with the outside world, which means that she controls practically all information. In houses that have opted for this model, the degree to which management is centralized depends on her aptitude for delegating tasks (outside contacts, projects, and administration).

Decisions and the basic ideological orientation of the house are communicated directly by the manager, who acts either alone or with the board of directors. Each member of the group has clearly defined tasks, making it less likely that staff will switch jobs around or combine several different roles. This way of operating is accepted and taken for granted.

Boards of directors are compulsory for non-profit organizations subsidized by the state, and this is where institutional influence first gains a foothold. The board is a collection of local professionals, business people, activists and intellectuals — whose common denominator is their connection with unions or social, legal, educational or health institutions.

Although the early boards of directors were mostly window-dressing, they were eventually replaced with boards that became extensively involved in all aspects of decision-making and orientation in the houses, reducing the sphere of internal management to the bare essentials. They even interfered in internal matters, although without creating any real problems. In the semi-institutional solution, there is very strong cohesion and little disagreement between the manager and the board of directors. This is undoubtedly partly due to the persons recruited, but the basic reason is the mutual belief in an institutional model, and hence interest in finding institutional solutions.

The semi-institutional solution is the most removed from the domestic model. Power relations are not diffuse; lines of authority are highly visible. This borrowing from the institutional pattern may reflect a desire to be incorporated into an official network, a search for professional recognition and, above all, a desire to avoid challenging existing services. This view dismisses the domestic model as a valid terrain for organizing the fight against conjugal violence, and ignores the idea of combining the domestic and public spheres:

> The *liberatory* affirmation of the traditionally devalued female aspects of life...is, of course, an extremely difficult task. For it requires a dynamic, critical and creative perspective which includes transformation in the very moment of affirmation.[13]

The attempt at an anarchist model

In the anarchist model,[14] communication is by successive consensus reached after debating the more or less fundamental issues involved in the orderly operations of the house. The group maintains an egalitarian discourse that may not faithfully reflect the varying capacities of different members to influence group decisions.

In this model, the co-ordinator is basically a functional role — *someone* has to deal with other groups and outside agencies. Internal organization is decentralized to a greater or lesser extent, and each staff person recognizes that they have equal jobs. The basic value in this alternative model is solidarity, and through solidarity they try to treat all women equally and reduce any hierarchical gap between the women seeking shelter and those providing it.

Information is controlled by the group as a whole. No one person is in charge of relations with outside groups or agencies, or acts as the sole representative for the group. Different women may take turns acting or speaking on behalf of the group, as long as they respect the mandate they receive from the group. Decisions are reached by consensus, following discussions that are sometimes lengthy and difficult. Ideological dissension is tolerated up to a certain point, and the expression of opposition is acceptable.

All movements need a utopian ideal, and the women's shelters movement is no exception. The anarchist model is rooted in the myth of 'sisterhood' or the "great dream of women's unity."[15] The utopian ideal is very much alive, reflected in the disproportion of women's expectations and the beauty of the harmonies achieved:

> We expect so much from a women's group, we want so much for it to be a radically different kind of group: a place where we can be ourselves, where we can share our questions, where we can count on total support when things are difficult for us, where children have a place, where complete democracy is obviously the rule, where there is no overwhelming leadership, where we can stretch ourselves to our limits, etc.[16]

Women's houses need this ideal in order to create something new and different, although the question of power remains the major source of contradiction for women. However, anyone who has belonged to a women's group and experienced the sense of total responsibility dependent solely on the solidarity of the other women will realize that something has changed:

> For the women who had worked to make their conception a reality, the experience of creating Transition House was one which validated their feminist beliefs. With no help from men, they had seen a need, devised a pragmatic and workable scheme for fulfilling the need, and had seen their plans become reality... Now the actualization of their goal increased their confidence and affirmed their conception of themselves and of other women, as competent, authoritative people... They are aware that the house exists because of the will, energy and abilities of a group of women.[17]

In a society in which only the male model of leadership is recognized, women are finding ways of working as a group without this kind of leadership.

Regardless of the specific way they choose to function or the utopian ideal underlying their choice — and the anarchist model is part of this ideal — women are seeking to handle power in a different way. They want to humanize it, to make power relations horizontal instead of vertical, to empower the group as a whole, with all the expectations and problems that this entails.

As the utopian symbol of the shelter movement, the anarchist model is the most valid approach to the problem of conjugal violence. The authority of the women providing shelter can only stem from their own solidarity with the women seeking shelter, women suffering from the abuse of power. Anarchy is the only really viable approach to power in a house for battered women.

The houses that try to operate on an anarchist model are those that apply the domestic model of organization the most faithfully. Power relations are diffuse, just as they are in the family model. Is this innovative, or does it simply reinforce the traditional status of women? It all depends on how the model is adapted and reworked. Is there a concern to verbalize it and make it apparent? Is it intuitively used as a valid way of putting an end to abuses of power?

Which houses are run on the anarchist model? To start with, all those run by women's collectives. It goes without saying that in these houses

> There is no boss or supervisor... although a woman may take a leadership role in a particular circumstance.[18]

Similarly, "non-hierarchical decision-making"[19] is practically a basic qualification for working in these collectives.

The radical experiences of these collectives are viewed with interest and shared to a lesser extent by many of the houses. They adopt some features of collective decision-making, without eliminating all hierarchical aspects of management. In such houses, the co-ordinator is open and accessible, seeks advice, and delegates work. It is relatively easy to take initiative.

Special attention is paid to the battered, dominated woman who, paradoxically, will look for authority structures as soon as she arrives at the shelter, clinging to them as a source of security.

While the hierarchical structures are real, they are seen as a form of co-operation among women, in which what is most important is to help each other: if women help each other, they will have no need to perpetuate dominator/dominated relations. The admiration that women still have for men — the physical, monetary, cultural or intellectual admiration that is the refined counterpart to the violent domination suffered by some women — withers once women acquire this fundamental experience of self-help.

Power struggles

A number of houses are currently in the process of replacing the semi-institutional solution with an attempt to operate on the anarchist model. It must be kept in mind that the houses are evolving and the models are not always applied in their extreme forms. Houses that started out as mini-institutions are borrowing more and more from the anarchist model. Others, founded along the most promising anarchist lines, are adopting some aspects of the institutional model and gradually becoming more structured. Actual houses do not fit neatly into any of the categories, and hybrids are quite common. Some houses have an authority structure that is visible to the staff but not to the residents. For women who are very dependent on men, this apparent absence of power may be a source of insecurity, but it also allows them to discover new models of responsibility.

The underlying principle of the teams in all the houses seems to be the same: homogeneity. Each group, each house, is built around criteria of similarity that often are not explicitly stated. Each house has one overriding criterion that shapes and characterizes its general outlook. There are teams of housewives, or feminists, or highly educated, well-off women, or university graduates, or nuns... Each house tends to preserve the homogeneity of the group involved. If two different tendencies were combined, the stronger one would eventually impose its vision of the house. A very homogeneous team will not experience these shifts in power.

These shifts can change the orientation of the house at any stage. They may occur during or after the founding period. They may be instigated by staff or by members of the board of directors. Can they be sparked by residents? In houses in Québec, the residents do not enjoy enough power to generate change. The situation in Great Britain is very different, however. There, the houses provide long-term shelter to women who run the houses themselves. This model has not been generally retained in the Canadian experience.

These shifts in power undermine existing leadership and reveal new leaders. They bring out the forces at play within the group. They also reveal diffuse power structures and highlight a reality with which women tend to be unfamiliar — power struggle.

Making room for children

When women create their own places or their own services, they often do it in a family framework. the first steps outside the house resemble a meeting of neighbours. Relations are extended family relations. This natural trend is described at length by Marilyn French in her first novel:

> Otherwise, it was an uneventful summer. The children were around all the time. The women had long learned to sit through the humid days with iced tea, listening to child noises.[20]

Women's houses respect women's habit of meeting while at the same time keeping track of the children's comings and goings. These women are neither relatives nor neighbours, but the same mechanism is at work here in bringing them together. In the houses, new ties are often established over a cup of coffee while keeping an eye on the children. The women share a common experience of violence, but they are also women defined by the fact that they have children and are mothers.

Children as part of women's celebration

In the midst of crisis, right after the blows and the injuries, only one thing matters for a woman: her children. She hopes they didn't see, don't realize. She didn't scream for fear of waking them... they are here with her now. She has snatched them away from God knows what storm, taking them with her to face an unknown future. They are all together at the shelter. They cling to each other.

In her desperate flight from the conjugal home, a woman leaves everything — her spouse, the father of her children, her home, her personal belongings, her social identity, her standing with relatives — everything. But she still has her children. Her status as a mother provides the starting point for building a new identity:

> Everyone knows that women, as a group, have an exaggerated sense of responsibility and guilt feelings about their children. Indeed, everything contributes to sustaining these feelings so as to keep women in the specific roles to which they have been assigned. Although their opinion has never been asked, it has always been assumed that a woman lives for love, and that her existence revolves around conceiving and raising children.[21]

A woman exists through her children. Often she decides to come to the shelter because of them, because of their reactions. They are also the reason she decides to start legal action to end the violence. Women's insistence on identifying themselves in terms of their children is comprehensible given that children are "the only thing they produce that society recognizes as valid."[22]

And men know this — their first tactic is always to threaten to deprive the mother of custody. Women have a chronic, gut fear of losing custody and the social disapproval this entails. A mother without custody is a bad mother. A father who does not have legal custody is not similarly judged; he is merely a man with better things to do than to look after children, even his own.

Although it is rare for a woman in a shelter to lose legal custody of her children or to have them kidnapped by her husband, when it does happen it always causes great turmoil. This attack on her identity is a painful experience shared by all the women who support her. She feels excluded from the women's celebration in getting together to watch the children play.

A new social practice

Vulnerable, victims of parental violence, and then of the separation, children have always been of special concern for staff in the shelters. More and more of the houses' programmes and activities are devoted to them. In the beginning, the houses saw the woman as their priority. They did not want to succumb to the institutional pitfall of allotting huge budgets to children while overlooking the real social causes of their problems. Spawned by the women's movement, the shelter movement quite rightly focused on the fate of the woman who was in practice ignored by society. The budgets and professional workers already devoted to troubled children certainly justified choosing this complementary work.

But the actual experience of transition houses with the child witnesses of family violence led them to rethink their practices: "We have had to rethink the entire question of the child's stay here."[23] Procedures designed to make children feel safe and at ease have been developed, along with ways of continuing their schooling. Times for conversations and games encouraging them to express their feelings are promoted. For instance, many houses set aside certain walls for free painting, and each group of children can paint as they wish. A few houses have even begun children's meetings to discuss house rules, personal concerns and conflicts among the children. The children are given explanations of "the legal terms used by their mothers that often frighten them. For example: going to court, seeing the lawyer, and above all, custody of the children."[24] Sports programmes channel their aggressivity, and the children are often invited to take part in organized activities that keep them away from television and the violence of the media. When possible, they are put into contact with young male child-care workers with whom they establish relationships of trust.

For the same reasons, other houses have set up parent/children courses aimed at directly affecting the mother/child relationship. The courses are taken by women who have left the shelters as a way of continuing the process begun during their stay in the houses.[25]

Whatever the specific way this concern for the child is expressed, women's houses have broken new ground in social work by taking in both mother and children. There was nothing in the administrative rules of social institutions to provide for this kind of work. Even now, the debate over the respective roles of the Ministry of Social Affairs, social welfare and the social service centres (CSSs) reflects the administrative imbroglio into which various institutions and administrative levels have been plunged by the shelters' very existence and right to survive.

Providing shelter for several women and their children at the same time encouraged the emergence of new ways of taking charge and collectivizing tasks. The fundamental principle of collective responsibility in the women's houses has meant that they have been able to provide residents of the shelters with day care and support and information services that were gained outside, in the rest of society, only after long struggles. This new practice of no longer separating women and their children is both the fruit of women's solidarity and a source of renewed solidarity.

Space defines practice

To truly understand the originality practised in women's houses, the organization of space in the houses must be analyzed. The 'material feminists' believed that women should have economic, social and environmental control of their own work. Since the environment should reflect women's equality, space, too, must be analyzed. Domestic space is a social product. In a capitalist world built around individual enterprise, domestic architecture is considered a private rather than a collective matter. But women's domestic work is essential to the working of the system and used by men for their own profit.[26]

The purpose of women's houses, as we have seen, is to overcome women's isolation. This implies offering the women a new kind of domestic space. In many cases, however, projects were begun on a shoestring and had to accept or rent houses that did not really correspond to what they needed. Women's houses are lodged in premises ranging from institutions to renovated urban housing to suburban homes. The staff did not always have a choice about the original premises, but as they began to get subsidies many houses have been able to move out of decrepit buildings into more permanent quarters. The opportunity to choose the premises is important for the autonomy of the centre's work.

In a number of regions, the fact that the centre was located in a big institution has had unfortunate consequences for its autonomy. The staff in these houses have no say in the choice of their clientèle: public services (the police and social services) turn over people picked up in all kinds of situations night and day. After all, they have to be put somewhere! There have been cases where a battered woman was sheltered on the first floor of a house while her husband was taken in on the second floor for some other problem. It is difficult for houses to define their own practices in these conditions.

Other, more institutional houses create a fictitious family environment in an effort to remedy at least some of the effects of institutional architecture. Many stay in an institutional setting either because they have no alternative or because they do not realize how the problem and environmental factors are related.

In contrast, in houses that are too small, contacts between the families and women staff are closer, and relations are warmer, more informal and more family-like.

The recent acquisition of some big single-family urban houses has enabled a few teams to reorient their work. Bigger houses allow them to take in more families simultaneously, and the additional children require that one or more child-care workers be hired. This first step towards the liberation of these women calls for other areas of liberation — from housework, cooking, and so on. Gradually, the residents' discourse

67

changes. Autonomy, which initially consisted of retaining responsibility for the children and developing shared responsibility with the other families, now also includes consciousness-raising and steps towards a new stage in life with or without the spouse.

The new domestic space

The woman housed in a women's shelter is introduced to a new experience — the communal house. Well-educated or economically comfortable women are at first often reluctant to share in such living arrangements, but shed their hesitations when they discover the solidarity and enduring friendships created with the other women in the house.

During their stay in a transition house, women spend a lot of time in communal spaces like the kitchen, living room, laundry room, children's playroom and meeting room. Most of the houses insist on a single communal table in the kitchen. While the use of individual tables would respect the family's privacy, it would not foster contact among the women.

This organization of space is a small-scale repetition of the attempts by 'material feminists' at the turn of the century to socialize domestic work by developing a "domestic architecture on a collective rather than a private basis."[27] Dolores Hayden is convinced that the shelter movement has the same ideological roots:

> Only a few activists who staffed refuges for battered women and their children had begun to question traditional housing design.[28]

Shelters also have semi-collective spaces, or family spaces, namely, the bedrooms. Each family thus retains its privacy; and if problems arise in their relations with other residents they can withdraw temporarily. A woman and child who make only partial use of a room may, after consultation, agree to share it with another woman and child. Since the women's house is a shelter, all the women understand the urgency of other women's situations. Women who were very lonely before coming to the shelter readily accept the collective approach to tasks.

The myth of the 'queen of the home' is challenged and replaced by a new value, the collectivization of housework. Three women can actually bake a cake together without any problem of co-ordination.

Office space

Office space is the third kind of space in women's houses. Almost non-existent in some houses, it is overwhelming, even all-pervasive in others. Office space is a counterpart to domestic space, although it cannot really be described as complementary. Domestic space could exist without office space, and vice versa.

The office — be it a single desk or a room — is a most revealing indicator of the orientation of the house. Houses that tend towards or have opted for semi-professionalism have several rooms with desks or a number of desks in one or adjoining rooms.

In our society, the desk is the ultimate symbol of the bureaucratic system. It symbolizes the middle- and upper-class illusion that social problems can always be managed by writing them away. All solutions to social problems entail the development of gigantic bureaucracies: unemployment insurance, social welfare, and social services. The very first move of any new employee in this system is to be shown his/her desk — his/her mooring point.

In a women's house, the desk always seems out of place in what is domestic space. Its significance may vary, depending on how the staff wish to use it. If the desk is reserved for the sole use of one person, it is located in the manager's, or the secretary's, or the social worker's office. Such an arrangement indicates advanced specialization. If the only desk in the house is in a small room, all the staff take turns using it. It is also a multi-purpose piece of furniture. It becomes a place to put the baby during an interview, or a telephone table for the residents. It often serves as the hub of the house, where women and children arrive and leave. If the desk is in the middle of the room, it may become a dividing line between the staff providing shelter and the residents. For this reason, a number of houses have located their desks along the walls of the office. As well as saving space in small rooms, this arragement subtly emphasizes the assigned role of the office — to take care of a minimum of written and administrative reports. An office room has the advantage of providing a closed space for private interviews. But here again, there is a serious risk of drifting away from collective practice into individual casework.

Two factors contribute simultaneously to the extension of space in the houses. The purchase of new, bigger houses provides more space; and upgrading or retraining of personnel raises academic requirements and leads to professional standards. The amount of administrative work expands enough to keep several members of the staff busy either full-time or part-time. Houses are growing in many different ways all at once, and the new shelters have often evolved a long way from the original houses.

What effect will this have? And how can each change be correctly weighed and judged in terms of the overall evolution of the shelter movement? I do not have any definitive answers to these questions; at best I can suggest a few hypotheses as provisional answers.

Two feminist trends

Shelters are a social, economic and environmental reaction to the condition of women, a direct descendant of socializing and communitarian feminism. The women who staff them, however, are for the most part a different kind of feminist. For want of a better term, I shall call them 'contemporary feminists.'

In Montréal, the houses are staffed by middle-class women, many of whom have college or university degrees. They share a number of attitudes characteristic of contemporary feminism:
— they accept the design of the single-family house or private apartment;
— they have no clear policy on unpaid housework;
— they negotiate the division of work with men (analyzing housework in terms of time rather than the spatial design of household arrangements);[29]
— they readily believe that equality depends on women's capacity to replace men in the system of production or services.

The contradiction between the shelter workers' private lives and values and the organization of their work leads to a new dilemma. Dilemmas are certainly nothing new for women, and Louise Vandelac talked about 'social schizophrenia' in her opening speech to the conference on Women, Health and Power.[30] All these features of contemporary feminism are more or less contradictory with the communal dimensions of women's houses. It is this contradiction that explains their evolution towards a semi-institutional format in which versatility in multiple tasks and skills is replaced by a division between manual and intellectual work; where informal intervention is formalized in professional interviews; where the organizational format borrows from related institutions, paving the way for a form of civil-servant mentality and its counterpart, unionization.

However well-adapted these borrowings from male institutions may be, they will never be the solution to the growing pains of women's houses. They do suggest, however, that solutions derived from a female model will have less and less influence in the houses. Does this reflect women's ambivalence, working out structures in which they can feel secure, with well defined rights, specialized tasks and clearly identified co-ordinators? This explanation, related to the socialization of women, calls for further research. Women have been socialized to be accommodating, protected by structures, submissive *vis-à-vis* an outside order. But the founding of the women's houses was an initiative that contradicted their socialization, a fact that should not be glossed over or lost from sight in an overly rigid explanation.

Or perhaps this should be seen as the evolution of an organization in which reality tends more and more to be structured by rationality (the male choice). The tools developed in recent years are increasingly important. Versatility and multiple tasks do not leave time for digging into all aspects of the problem. Innovators naturally want to develop their first intuitions more fully, and after the early work of founding houses may feel a new urgency about being free to organize, research and publicize their findings. Freeing them for this new work inevitably means changes in the staff teams that make the work and tasks more unequal, marring women's dream of equality.

Conclusion

The domestic model of organization is thus very important in women's houses. For Sheriff and Campbell, it resembles the model of the small family business in which there is
— minimal specialization of tasks;
— co-ordination as part of all tasks;
— no precise definition of rights and obligations;
— strong dedication to general goals;
— no rigidly defined hierarchy;
— a predominance of advice and horizontal communication.[31]

In the beginning, the houses did have these characteristics, but few have succeeded in retaining this simplicity of operations. The organization of the houses has become more and more complex as the demands of their partners in the social affairs network have become more complex.

Regardless of the interest of this model, however,

> ...where power is shared, the (dominant) ideology is sufficiently strong to persuade researchers to consider these organizations as incidental variations or undesirable phenomena within capitalist society dedicated to efficiency. Their marginality makes them tolerable, but they have no possibility of becoming predominant in the near future.[32]

In contrast, "the male model of rationality and reason implicitly dominates our conception of optimal organization."[33]

In the long run, if the family business model borrows too heavily from the rational model we will wind up with women's houses run by and for women using tools that are increasingly foreign to women's values. This paradox would gradually destroy the alternative nature of the houses.

The merit of women's houses is to have sparked a pragmatic debate on the status of women in general. It is not a debate about domestic production versus commodity production. It is not a debate between feminists and anti-feminists, or working women and housewives. All these oppositions derive from the male standards that continue to divide and isolate women. The heart of the debate is the challenge to the domestic model of organization women have known. But the debate cannot take place unless actual examples of a modified approach exist.

As they evolve, women's words and women's actual collective practice in networks of solidarity are confronted with other models permeated by rationality. Is it possible to achieve a synthesis of these two trends?

Already we have seen that the organization changes as professional and scientific dimensions are introduced. Under the impact of these other models, what will happen to the domestic structures considered indispensable to working out solutions that meet women's needs?

Notes

1. On this, see Ginette Larouche, *Une étude sur la violence conjugale,* Université de Montréal, 1981.
2. Lorraine Godard, *Document de travail du colloque de Longueuil,* December 3-4, 1977, pp. 5-12.
3. Canadian Advisory Council on the Status of Women, Government of Canada, "L'organisation de la maison de transition de Régina," conference of March 5-7, 1980, p. 22.
4. Confédération des syndicats nationaux, one of the three major union federations in Québec.
5. Lorraine Godard, *op. cit.*
6. Roxanne Simard, *Va te faire soigner, t'es malade!* Stanké, 1981, pp. 89-90.
7. Claire Harting, "Un film où les femmes jouent leur propre personnage," *Journal de Montréal,* February 18, 1982.
8. Angela Miles, "Le féminisme parole authentique et autonome des femmes," *Femmes et Politique,* Le Jour, 1981, p. 78. A slightly different version of this article has been published in English in Angela Miles and Geraldine Finn, eds., *Feminism in Canada: From Pressure to Politics.* Montréal: Black Rose Books, 1982, pp. 213-227.
9. Erin Pizzey, *Scream Quietly or the Neighbours Will Hear.* Harmondsworth, England: Penguin Books, 1974, p. 130.
10. *Ibid.*
11. Transition House, *A Study of Battered Women.* Vancouver, 1976, p. 9.
12. Erin Pizzey, *op. cit.,* p. 131.
13. Angela Miles, *op. cit.,* p. 72.
14. The expression 'anarchist model' has no political connotations here. It refers to a working hypothesis for exploring a certain refusal of order and hierarchy as a preliminary to creating new styles of management and administration in women's groups.

15. Le Théâtre des cuisines, *As-tu vu? Les maisons d'emportent!* Éditions du Remue-ménage, 1980, pp. 90-91.
16. *Ibid.*
17. Jillian Ridington, "The transition process: a feminist environment as reconstitutive milieu," *Victimology: An International Journal*, Vol. 2, 1977-78, p. 566.
18. Transition House, *op. cit.*, p. 9.
19. Jillian Ridington, *op. cit.*, p. 566.
20. Marilyn French, *The Women's Room.* New York: Harcourt, Brace, Jovanovich, 1977, p. 188.
21. Micheline Carrier, *Contre la violence,* June 1981.
22. *Ibid.*
23. Centre Refuge Montréal, *Rapport d'activités,* June 1981. (This centre is now known as the Refuge Multi-femmes.)
24. *Ibid.*
25. L'Escale pour Elle (Montréal), *Rapport d'activités,* June 1981.
26. Dolores Hayden, *The Grand Domestic Revolution.* Cambridge, Mass.: MIT Press, 1981, P. 8.
27. *Ibid.*, p. 50.
28. *Ibid.*, p. 294.
29. *Ibid.*
30. Anne Richer, *La Presse,* Montréal, May 22, 1982.
31. P. Sheriff and E.J. Campbell, "La place des femmes: dossier sur la sociologie des organisations," *Sociologie et Sociétés,* PUM, Vol. 13, No. 2 (October 1981), p. 127.
32. *Ibid.*, p. 128.
33. *Ibid.*

4

IDEOLOGICAL ORIENTATIONS OF VARIOUS TYPES OF SHELTERS

Now that we have some idea of the origins of the women's shelter movement and have shown the originality of the domestic model, we shall discuss in this chapter the different types of shelters and their ideological orientations (see Table 2[1]).

Two main ideological orientations can be seen within the movement concerning violence against women. The first is essentially concerned with protection. Within this general orientation, two subgroups can be identified: 'pure protectionists' and 'legal protectionists.' The second main orientation is essentially concerned with 'liberation'. This orientation can again be subdivided in terms of moderates and radicals.

These approaches will be discussed in more detail shortly, but reference must be made here to a recent article by Freda Paltiel:

> In addressing the problem, however, one is confronted by different ideological definitions of the problem, traditionalist, reformist, the pathological/therapeutic and that of the radical feminists which defines sexism as the oppression of women by men and therefore sees violence against women as the natural outgrowth of marriage, an institution in which men legally dominate women.[2]

Of course, these four approaches to the problem of violence against women are not restricted solely to the shelter movement. They are present whenever this problem is seriously addressed whether it be by social workers, government agencies or the population in general. In fact, each group develops its own approach and tries to promote it within the formal and informal networks involved. Radical ideas and grass-root experience mutually influence each other, thereby enriching the overall potential of the movement.

The protectionist approach is most prevalent in a traditional milieu. The women in this type of shelter are primarily concerned with providing protection and help for battered women and have not developed a social analysis of their experience.

Legal protectionists offer services on the basis of the rights of women who are victims of violence. The struggle for recognition of these rights is seen as an important part of helping to change their situation.

The idea of women's rights within marriage is still recent. Marriage — 'for better or for worse' — which could mean being abused by one's husband, being given a violent beating when he was drunk, for instance, no longer enjoys much public support:

> Less directly, the new focus on wife abuse is associated with a shift in values; it is no longer considered 'right' to endure any indignity to preserve a marriage.[3]

In addition to this protectionist orientation, there is what we have called the 'liberationist' orientation. Here, one is confronted with an eternal dilemma: should one attempt to be the spokesperson for the victims or should the priority be on helping these women to speak up for themselves? The liberationist orientation emphasizes the goal of autonomy for women who are temporarily in need of assistance. Most observers would agree that it is impossible for a woman to break out of the cycle of violence by herself. The liberationists seek to offer real but short-term solidarity which can allow victims to take steps towards changing their lives.

The moderate liberationists emphasize autonomy by involving women in self-help services. Their approach includes an analysis of power relations between men and women.

Finally, the radical liberationists, described above by Freda Paltiel, seek a radical transformation of society and relations between men and women.

> The revolutionary perspective in radical feminism involves a critique of contemporary forms of marriage and the family as they affect the sexual, economic, political and ideological oppression of women.[4]

All typological frameworks simplify reality, and this is clearly the case for the framework proposed here. Several factors must be considered, including the origins of the shelters, their evolution, the struggles which moved them closer or farther away from a particular orientation, the influence of the boards of directors, changes in personnel, urban or rural settings, and so forth.

Nevertheless, these factors tend to be interrelated, and the influence of a group, sometimes even of an individual, tends to give an overall picture of the shelter as shown in Table 2. This is due to the fact that the modes of operation are usually related to the general objectives of the shelter, which are, in turn, related to a more or less conscious ideology concerning services.

The clinical or therapeutic approach which seeks to provide specialized services for battered women is found most frequently in groups with a 'legal protectionist' or 'moderate liberationist' orientation. The pure protectionists do not wish to develop a scientific approach because of the social barriers which this type of approach involves for them. Generally speaking, these women are not university-trained and rely more on their own experience. The radical liberationists, for their part, go in a sense beyond the scientific approach which they tend to view critically even if, on occasion, they find it useful to have trained personnel on hand.

Service ideologies

The fact that the women's shelter movement grew out of the women's movement in general and that feminists played an active part in getting the shelters started means that several different traditions affect the way services are provided. In Québec, in particular, where the Catholic Church has had a strong influence on most public services, one quarter of these shelters are run by religious orders. Housewives and feminists are involved in the remainder. These three groups, which offer three different orientations, three modes of analysis and three traditions of services, make for considerable diversity within the movement. All shelters are confronted with the daily reality of women and all share the new and essentially feminist concern that violence is unacceptable: something must be done to help women who are victims of violence.

These three groups, however, have markedly different ideologies and draw upon radically different traditions. The housewives and nuns have a long tradition of providing services, whereas the feminists have new and different reference points. This ideological factor is of the utmost importance when we consider the daily operations of a shelter. Even if the feminist influence on organization within the shelters is most obvious, our analysis has shown references to more traditional models as well.

These three groups are not perceived in the same way and do not occupy the same status within the structures which have come into being. The feminists, who took the initiative of setting up and organizing the shelters, constitute the main reference point. The other groups, which maintain a lower profile, are referred to less often but are nevertheless present and exert a real influence. The combination of these groups and the various types of shelters gives an impression of considerable diversity.

The religious orders

Before 1960, the religious orders were responsible for providing basic social needs — education, health and welfare — on a private basis. What appears, in 1960, to have been a monopoly of the Church was, in part, the result of a century of personal commitment. The process of institutionalization, however, took on ever-greater proportions and eventually required state intervention:

> [The religious orders] controlled the vast majority of the institutions: hospitals, hospices, orphanages, juvenile delinquent centres, and so forth, as well as social work agencies and community centres. They were also responsible for the training and hiring of social work and paramedical personnel. Through charity drives and direct parish contributions, they contributed a crucial part of the financial resources necessary to maintain the health and welfare system.[5]

The sixties were a turning point for the religious orders when the Boucher Report officially sanctioned the trend towards professionalism in the areas of health, education and welfare.

> The Boucher Report attributed the primary role in the welfare sector to the state which acted in the name of social justice rather than public charity as before.[6]

81

This declaration that the ideal of social justice should replace the ethic of charity constituted public recognition of the right to assistance, independently of the causes of need.

The crisis which ensued struck at the heart of the religious orders. The ranks of these groups grew older and membership declined drastically, thereby accentuating a crisis which was, in essence, political.

> The Hospital Act of 1962 had the effect of expropriating the role of the religious communities within the hospitals.[7]

The religious orders were keenly aware of the political nature of the trend underway:

> The rejection of the religious orders during the sixties was, in part, a political phenomenon. It was at this time that the state passed laws enabling it to take control of all major institutions. Since we needed financial assistance if we were to keep pace with the reform, this inevitably meant state involvement.[8]

The crisis had important consequences for the orientations involved in the services offered by the religious orders. Faced with the threat of extinction, the religious institutions went through a process of serious soul-searching in an attempt to rediscover their original ideals and objectives. This led to discussion on a key question: Who are the dispossessed?

Without making specific reference to the feminists who had begun setting up women's shelters, the religious orders did come to see these houses as a modern priority in line with their tradition of service. This tradition had long been characterized by work with the dispossessed and women, particularly widows, unwed mothers, "elderly women living in poverty"[9] as well as the education of young women. All this, of course, had been undertaken without specific reference to the condition of women.

Many of the founders of religious orders were widows. They had thus been housewives who had experienced family life before they opened their homes to the needy of the day.

How does this compare with the women's shelters run by nuns today? There are, in fact, as many orientations as there are groups involved: there are traditionally oriented houses and more modern ones, some more open to external influences, others more closed, some have highly centralized organizational procedures, other more decentralized. Sometimes the board of directors is controlled by the religious orders, sometimes it is not. Some have developed a feminist approach, others a professional approach. Some are specifically oriented to a certain type of 'client,' others have no specific criteria at all.

This type of shelter has as many choices to face as the other types, and the fact that in some cases these houses have been turned over to other women (housewives or feminists) does not make their future any easier.

The ideal of 'social justice' which came to the forefront during the sixties is, in fact, a modern translation of the traditional notion of charity. The houses run by the religious orders respond to this need and are largely motivated by this ideal. For the most part, the houses run by the religious orders tend to be protectionist. Some of them borrow certain traits from the moderate liberationists but their organization is not based on the objective of autonomy for women.

Housewives

Who are the housewives? In general, they are women who are either presently (or were until recently) involved in bringing up a family. They generally do not have a university education although some of them have returned to their studies or are presently working in the labour market. These women have acquired considerable influence through volunteer work and social commitment and for these reasons have come to work in women's shelters. Their action can be defined in contrast to feminist struggles:

> ...These struggles... have not allowed women to identify more clearly their interests as women and housewives, nor have they encouraged collective action based on a new consciousness that

would enable them to undertake other struggles and become involved in a process of radical transformation of their living and working conditions. The feminists, therefore, do not consider these struggles as part of the feminist heritage.[10]

This distinction is important if we are to understand the ideology of housewives concerning services. The majority of the women's shelters operate on a model put forth by the housewives, which is largely influenced by the protectionist orientation.

Housewives often have a lifestyle close to that of the women seeking refuge. Their economic situation and their experiences as women are similar. How does this shared experience influence their efforts in changing situations related to the family?

Since she has been socialized to care for and to 'serve,' the service ideology of the housewife is cast in the mould of family life. As a child, she looked after her brothers and sisters; as an adult, she looks after her husband and children; and often, as time goes on, she looks after her parents, the handicapped or other elderly persons in the family. If life had cast her in a lower social class she would likely be a maid with the responsibility of looking after someone else's children and family.

Before social roles were called into question and the specificity of the conditions of women was analyzed, few women were able to escape this situation. Even those who were trained professionally generally served the sick, the young or the handicapped.

> Whereas before, the women in the family looked after the member of the family who was mentally retarded or elderly, today a woman is called upon to look after many deviants at once but now her work has become specialized so that she only looks after one category of deviants... It is now a 'science' rather than part of a life experience.[11]

The housewife is also a 'mystique' as Betty Friedan so powerfully pointed out. She is "the Happy Housewife Heroine."[12] She experiences the sense of isolation described earlier.

For this Alice in Wonderland, each street of a neighbourhood or village is a long corridor of walls and housewives. It is in part because of this solitude that we find her involved in community groups in an attempt to fulfill her own new needs outside the home once her children have left.

There are thus several issues which separate housewives from feminists. The struggles of women are different from feminist struggles even if they tend to converge in the long run.

> According to a survey conducted by AFEAS,[13] more than 70% of members polled declared themselves feminist even if almost 62% of them favoured only minor changes in society. Is this not contradictory?... This part of the survey was a real revelation for us. Five years ago, even the leaders of AFEAS would have shied away from calling themselves feminists. That gives us some indication of the immense changes that have occurred for members of AFEAS recently. But when these women were asked if they hoped their daughters would live the same type of life as they had lived, they replied that their life was not so bad. It is not easy for women to imagine a society in which they would enjoy equal opportunity, a society in which they would have the positions they merit. Women do not have an example to which they can refer when making up their minds. Since they often feel insecure in relation to the future, they tend to prefer more gradual change.[14]

Thus, the service ideology of housewives is not oriented towards social change or the transformation of the family structure. They attempt to 'look after' what exists.

Feminists

Housewives were the first feminists.[15] They were the ones who formulated a critique of the condition of women in contemporary society and sought to bring about change. But as feminist ideology became more radical, the definition of feminism narrowed. Not everyone who seeks improvements in the living and working conditions of women can be considered a feminist.

At the outset, feminist movements were essentially made up of housewives. Everything changed when a new, more radical generation arrived on the scene.[16]

Who are these radical women? Where did they come from? In general, they are highly educated and come from a very different social background than the housewives.

> Since these [groups] were campus-based, the participants tended to be young, single or childless and middle class as were most of the women involved in radical feminism throughout North America at that time.[17]

These young radical women came to the shelters via other struggles involving women's issues. Although comparatively few in number, feminist shelters have had a powerful effect on the others. The struggle for autonomy, which is the ideological basis of these shelters, has influenced in varying degrees the entire liberationist orientation.

The women's movement grew out of the political activism of youth in the sixties.

> In the late nineteen sixties... women who had been involved in radical organizations began to realize that they were experiencing oppression even in groups supposedly dedicated to seeking justice and relieving oppression.[18]

The transition to feminism from political activism in male-dominated groups was accomplished in part with the help of consciousness-raising groups on the one hand and active social commitment to women's causes on the other.

> Having realized their own oppression, the members of these first feminist groups had that reality confirmed through working with other women in 'consciousness-raising' sessions, or in the many special-interest groups which evolved from the original organizations.[19]

Feminists, then, do not have the tradition of 'service' as do the nuns and housewives but rather an ideology of struggle for the rights of the oppressed.

In Québec, feminists also came from other women's groups and struggles:

> The women who have been in the forefront of the struggle against violence and for women's shelters are often the same women who were active in struggles on such unpopular issues as the right to paid work, day-care centres, free contraception and abortion clinics, control over their own bodies, tax reform (still not achieved) and more equitable sharing of family resources and role definitions as well as access to all types of jobs. These women have also given active support to women involved in other struggles... Always ready to lend a helping hand on specific issues, to participate in demonstrations, these women were almost everywhere at once. At one point they decided to give priority to their efforts against violence principally because their experiences as women forced them to realize just how serious and how deeply rooted this problem is. They became convinced that physical, moral and psychological violence is one of the main obstacles preventing them from exercising their rights in the areas mentioned above. For this reason, they have concentrated their efforts on this issue.[20]

Feminist women's shelters are found mainly in Montréal, Québec, and on the North Shore. Their radical views have influenced many of the more moderate shelters, in particular concerning the question of the autonomy of women. Since their ideology is still perceived as radical, feminists are somewhat marginal in the women's shelter movement but their ideas are viewed with less apprehension now and alliances are being formed with the more moderate liberationists.

The first refuge for battered women was the idea of a feminist, supported by several housewives. Chiswick Women's Aid was the result of an interesting compromise.

> Though I was the only person in the group who was a feminist, all of us felt that the publicity that surrounded the Women's Lib movement put many women off.[21]

Erin Pizzey began Women's Aid with the help of women from her neighbourhood. Her co-workers were women who had serious problems such as alcoholism. Here, feminist ideology was put into practice with a group of housewives.

The feminist approach seeks to highlight the social dimensions of women's problems.

> To this end, Ishtar considers itself to be a 'feminist' organization; one that will provide women with the tools to see their own situations as being partly the product of society's attitudes toward women.[22]

The feminist orientation is essentially 'liberationist' in that it considers that a woman is not really protected until she can defend herself and gain economic and emotional independence.

These orientations, then, reflect the diversity of social and political views present in dealing with the everyday experiences of battered women.

The experiences of feminist women's shelters have an effect outside the feminist movement. Women from all walks of life with different backgrounds and values work out their own alternatives and discuss their own ideas and hopes in relation to the model put forth by the radical feminists.

The new arrivals in women's shelters are often somewhat removed from these ideological debates. They are young, college or university educated, and are unfamiliar with the living conditions typical of a housewife. The Quiet Revolution in Québec, the May '68 events in France, or the demonstrations against the war in Vietnam are not part of their own experience. For them, even feminists are part of a somewhat different generation. On the other hand, their lives are directly affected by the present economic crisis and they are keenly aware of the injustices of a situation which restricts their right to work and condemns them to various forms of under-employment. Their personal investments in education have not paid social dividends and they tend to see technical and scientific knowledge as a means of gaining social recognition. These young women, although relatively unknown and few in number at the present time, constitute the new type of candidate for employment in the shelters. In time, they could have a major influence in redefining the mission of the shelters in terms of scientific and professional criteria.

Four types of shelters

The two main ideological orientations generate four types of shelters, each of which has a relatively coherent set of ends and means. No single shelter can be seen as a pure example of one type, but on the whole, certain distinctive characteristics emerge. This portrait is shown in Table 2.

The objective of such a typology is to present an overall picture of the shelters and to show each type in relation to the others, thereby giving us some idea of the parameters of the movement. The complexity of analyzing violence against women and the responses to this problem (in terms of services and struggles) comes out clearly in this table.

The pure protectionists

The women involved in protectionist shelters do not have an explicit service ideology. Since their ideology is basically the same as the dominant ideology, they do not feel the need to justify it. Hélène David defines dominant ideology as "the totality of representations, values, norms and beliefs through which sexual and class domination is perpetuated."[23] The author goes on to explain the way in which dominant ideology masks reality:

> However, ideology also reflects the way people experience their conditions of existence and at this level it is so deeply ingrained in their activities that it is inseparable from their life experiences.[24]

Pure protectionists do not have a feminist analysis. In fact they have no articulated mode of analysis of their own. They simply fall back upon the clichés of dominant ideology and its beliefs concerning family, school, the state and the Church. They consider the nuclear, dual parent family as the basis of society. The moral imperative to 'look after' women in difficulty is thus a logical consequence of this social outlook.

Does this mean that the pure protectionists end up blaming the victims? Involuntarily, perhaps. Isn't this just what dominant ideology does? Victimization is a subtle process which seems, at first, to be 'humanitarian.'

It is already known that women who are victims of violence have a tendency to want to control their environment with the hope of avoiding further violence. They try to plan the times when the husband comes home, to manage the family budget so as not to be forced to ask for more money, to put the children to bed so they will not be disturbed by scenes of violence, to refrain from discussing problems with friends and family so as not to make things worse, and so forth. It is easy for a staff member to slip into these well established ways of thinking and to justify them in the name of family and parental responsibilities.

> ...the humanitarian can have it both ways. He can, all at the same time, concentrate his charitable interest on the defects of the victim, condemn the vague social and environmental stresses that produced the defect (some time ago), and ignore the continuing effect of victimizing social forces (right now). It is a brilliant ideology for justifying a perverse form of social action designed

to change, not society, as one might expect, but rather society's victim.[25]

In the pure protectionist shelters, there is no clear policy concerning the types of women to be admitted nor the approaches to be used. Many of these shelters have no clear mission: sometimes they accept women in difficulty, sometimes teen-age girls in trouble with the Youth Protection Board. At other times, the emphasis may shift towards 'bag-ladies' or ex-convicts or alcoholics. At times, there is a mixture of all these different types of women. All this, of course, comes under the vague heading of aiding 'women and children in difficulty.'

There is also the problem of self-perception of women who seek refuge in these shelters. How do they define their situation? In relation to which groups, role models, and types of analysis? In some shelters there is simply no answer to these questions or an answer that is so confused it tends to reinforce their present family roles.

The model of domestic organization is not used as a way of reaching out to these women. Paradoxically, it is the women who know this model best — but who have had little choice in this domain — who tend to minimize the importance of critical thought on domestic organization.

In the protectionist shelters, only the functional aspects of domestic life are considered. Participation of residents in the daily running of the shelter is discouraged and the staff is entirely responsible for services. These services are defined in similar ways to those offered by hospitals or social work agencies with a clear distinction between the women who help and the women who are helped. Control of the situation is thus ensured but the potential of residents is not tapped; there is an "absence of encouraging the spontaneous tendency for women to help each other out."[26]

The organizational procedures in protectionist shelters reinforce the tendency towards centralization of decision-making in the hands of a single individual (the director, often the founding director). A hierarchical structure often remains implicit even when a general spirit of harmony seems to prevail. The board of directors formally approves the decisions of the director and show fews signs of independence. The staff has few formal rights, and salaries tend to reflect this status. Interest in regional or provincial organizations is limited. The director and occasionally one other colleague attend these meetings.

The pure protectionist shelters, then, tend to faithfully duplicate the basic characteristics of the home environment of those women seeking refuge. Influences from other ideological models tend to be limited by virtue of the centralized and hierarchical control exercised in this type of shelter. Nevertheless, these shelters make an important contribution to the movement: their number and their representation carry weight in the eyes of the government.

The legal protectionists

Although these shelters are an outgrowth of the pure protectionists, they operate in substantially different ways in several areas. They share with the pure protectionists the difficulty in identifying their own ideological premises which in fact are generally concomitant with those of society as a whole.

Their outlook thus tends to be traditional but with a modern objective: new rights must be gained in order to further reform the condition of women. The women in this subgroup tend to have considerable social influence and exercise a prudent and conservative type of leadership. They tend to be relatively close to established political parties and have considerable organizational experience. They are often college trained and tend to favour hiring professional women to deal with the problems of women in difficulty.

Diane Lamoureux depicts this 'institutional' orientation in the following way:

> Faced with the failure of traditional family structures, this group attempts to define a new relationship between men and women while at the same time avoiding the issue of the oppression of women.[27]

Women, from this point of view, are seen as subjects who have rights which must be respected. Marriage is no longer an institution in which one has to accept one's fate. It is a contract in which rights are defined and exercised by both parties.

Legal protectionists do not see things in specifically feminist terms, but rather in terms of 'scientific' knowledge. They naturally tend to rely upon the state and the services it provides. Their social position often enables them to make profitable alliances with the established social structures and professional organizations.

For this reason, this type of shelter often resembles government-run institutions. On the whole, clients are admitted on the basis of a clear policy and often referred to more professional services. Procedures and methods used tend to favour an individual approach to problems. Knowledge of available resources is excellent and the services provided are of high quality.

The domestic model of organization is used and its main characteristics are well understood. Often the women involved in setting up this type of shelter have carefully studied the experience of similar shelters in the United States, Ontario and British Columbia and are thus able to incorporate the main characteristics of the domestic model of organization.

These shelters tend to try to combine two main approaches: one based on first-hand experience, the other on scientific knowledge. Patrician science tolerates plebian common sense. In this context, the domestic model of organization tends to be seen as little more than a family (and thus familiar) setting for women seeking refuge and not as a means of liberation as discussed above.

The organization of these shelters tends to be more flexible than those of the pure protectionist type although the inbred hierarchical values of these women tend to encourage spontaneous self-discipline. The degree of delegation of responsibilities and consultation varies according to the managerial style of the woman responsible for the shelter.

This type of shelter often employs women professionals who are employed by government social aid agencies or community clinics, 'on loan' to the shelter, or else women who have had previous employment in these institutions. The staff tends to work together closely when there is a single ideological orientation and outside influences are minimal. This fact, which is not surprising in the context of the protectionist orientation, can also be explained by the fact that the claims to absolute superiority voiced by professional practice are not generally accepted in the shelter movement and in fact are sometimes openly opposed by the 'liberationist' orientation.

The moderate 'liberationists'

The 'liberationist' orientation views with a critical eye the generally accepted ideas and values concerning women and the family. This critical eye is, of course, guided by a critical ideology. To break with dominant ideology necessarily involves formulating into words and conceptual systems a critique of dominant norms. The verbalization of this critical distance is a means of identifying the differences that women want to create.

There is a fundamental ideological difference between the liberationist and the protectionist orientations. Protectionists choose to create structures which emphasize security and comfort. Liberationists favour choice and independence. They attempt to reach out to women as a collective force.

The non-radical liberationist orientation can be further divided into three subgroups:

> ...Women's groups which stress the goal of equality of rights; [Second,] groups (open to both men and women) which are more or less marxist and which consider the issue of equality between two sexes to be related to struggle for economic and political power by a new social class, i.e., the working class; [thirdly,] every woman who, each in her own home, tries to change power relations in what is still seen as the sphere of *private life*.[28]

This type of shelter is not the most prevalent in Québec. It tends to be staffed by women who are active in citizen's groups or women's groups, legal activists, feminist social workers and women who have participated in consciousness-raising groups.

These shelters have a feminist approach and 'socialistic' concerns. Their analysis is based on contemporary feminist writings and their own direct and indirect experience of the feminist movement. This analysis is felt to be essential for their efforts in helping women to deal with the specific forms of violence confronting them. At the same time, however, a certain type of feminism is viewed critically. These women emphasize that the needs of poor women are not the same as others. (For example, to allow her to keep her maiden name does not change the material conditions of her life.)

The domestic model of organization is an essential part of these shelters and it is inconceivable that they could exist without this dimension. The life experiences of battered women are considered as extremely important. Priority is given to encouraging women to voice their concerns and all efforts are made to support this process of articulation. The residents are called upon to participate in all aspects of the life of the house: domestic life, mutual help between women, night duty for admission, decision-making concerning objectives, public education, workshops, and pressure tactics.

The internal organization of these shelters is based on the principle of self-reliance — by and for the residents. Responsibilities are clearly defined and shared collectively in small groups. Occasional leadership qualities are encouraged. Both formal and informal group 'therapy' is considered positively by the women involved in these shelters even though an individual approach is still seen as necessary. Advocacy tactics and support companionship of victims are used and considered essential. Public education and pressure group activities are seen as a necessary (and logical) complement to helping individual women.

The process of 'victimization' in all its complexity is seen by the liberationists as a key towards developing new strategies:

> In some ways victimization can and should be thought of in terms of 'survival.' Bettelheim points out that survival has to be divided into two aspects: (1) what the victim can do to survive (what he can do for himself and what others can do for him), and (2) what

the outside world can do to change the structural conditions that encourage victimization.[29]

Liberationists work towards setting up programmes based on the theory of victimization and "demand specific services, not ones which were meant for other people or other problems."[30]

The radical 'liberationists'

Should a study of women's shelters focus on radical theory and action? In a sense, this would be justified by the fact that this viewpoint has, as its primary objective, the autonomy of women, and the means used are a logical consequence of this objective.

Our concern here, however, has been to describe the women's shelter movement — as it exists. For this reason, it is important to understand the actions of all the women involved and not just those of the feminists.

Nevertheless, to examine the most radical forms of the reality under study is one of the most interesting aspects of research. The radical viewpoint is the only one which openly declares the main objective of the women's shelter movement: the autonomy of women. The shelters run by these women are few in number and tend to be somewhat marginal in relation to the movement as a whole.

Certain fundamental principles define the radical orientation of this viewpoint. What is at stake here is not the struggle for new rights but the struggle for a new society:

> Since radical feminism begins with the postulate of the antagonistic nature of relations between men and women, the objective is not so much to win new rights as to define new modes of social existence in which social relations will no longer be defined by men alone but by all individuals in society. In this way, radical feminism is not only a critique of patriarchal society but also a means through which new social relations can be explored and developed, in particular through solidarity amongst women.[31]

The phenomenon of victimization of women is seen by radical groups as symptomatic of the condition of women in general in much the same way that rape is seen as symptomatic of sexual oppression of women in society. The radical orientation seeks to encourage women to become aware of their oppression and tries to help them deal with this realization. It also attempts to show how the oppression of women is present in a multitude of aspects of their daily lives.

The radical activists are conscious of the importance of an active presence for these women and they are also aware of the resources which exist to help them, but at the same time they emphasize that the desire for change can only come from the women themselves. The radical groups do not say: "We will protect you," or "We will help you" but rather, "Things will change when you decide to face up to this problem and act." These groups speak for all women and not just individual victims of violence.

This goal of autonomy requires safeguards against the development of dependency and concrete strategies through which objectives can be achieved. The struggle to obtain collective control and responsibility for the shelters is seen as part of a more general struggle for women to gain control and responsibility for their own lives. First of all, one must learn how to live and be with women since the presence of men inevitably makes this struggle for independence more difficult. Secondly, the shelter must learn to rely on its own resources and to avoid placing its fate in the hands of some other institutional body (board of directors) which would make the shelter dependent on other people, other values and other perceptions of the problems at hand. When power is exercised by a small number of people, it is easier to make it accessible to women who have sought refuge and to adapt this power according to the needs of the shelter. Collective responsibility means that decisions are made according to the needs of those concerned.

The autonomous organization model proposes radical alternatives to mainstream models. The domestic organization model is used not to perpetuate how women live traditionally but rather as a form of subversion and as an alternative to solitude. These houses are not simply a place where one does housework (thereby perpetuating a negative image of the house) but rather a place where women can

Table 2

	PROTECTIONIST ORIENTATION		LIBERATIONIST ORIENTATION	
	Pure Protectionist	Legal Protectionist	Moderate Liberationist	Radical Liberationist
Ideology	The family is the basis of society. The violent and irresponsible behaviour of some men constitutes a threat to their wives and children.	The family is the basis of society, and women have rights — including the right not to be beaten.	The family is composed of power relationships between men and women. These relationships must be changed as part of an overall struggle for change in socio-economic conditions and against social inequality.	The nuclear family is a bourgeois institution. Women are victims of male oppression in patriarchal society. The phenomenon of battered women is symptomatic of the condition of women as a whole.
General objectives	To look after women in difficulty.	To help women and to encourage them to learn their rights.	To encourage women to become independent and to solve their problems by becoming aware of the place of women in society.	To involve women in a process of collective liberation. Their personal problems are the starting point for this process.
Socialization	Traditional values can provide help for the decisions and challenges facing these women.	Traditional values are supplemented with the notion of rights.	Traditional values are of little help in making the decisions and changes necessary.	Traditional values concerning women and the family must be radically criticised.

Alliances	Priority: Work in the shelter. Contact with radical feminists is avoided.	Priority: Work in the shelters and encourage women's culture and activities.	Priorities: Work in the shelters while at the same time developing conjunctural alliances (on the basis of group decisions) with women's groups and feminist activities.	Work directly and actively with other groups.
	Little analysis of relations with political institutions.	Little critical distance in relation to the ideology of existing government institutions.	The ideology of government institutions is seen critically and this critique is the subject of an ongoing process of reflection.	The political institutions are seen as part of the state apparatus in capitalist society which exercise social control.
Services vs. autonomy	Provide as many services as possible.	Quality of services provided is the primary objective, through specialized treatment if necessary.	Expand the notion of services to include the notion of autonomy.	Services are kept to a strict minimum in order to allow women to become involved in the collective struggle for a better life for women.
Organization	Hierarchical organization of power. Consultation is not binding on the director.	Hierarchical organization of power tempered by effective consultation.	Power tends to be distributed horizontally although co-ordination is recognized as necessary.	Power is distributed horizontally and procedures are developed by the group on the basis of consensus.

Table 2 (continued)

	PROTECTIONIST ORIENTATION		LIBERATIONIST ORIENTATION	
	Pure Protectionist	Legal Protectionist	Moderate Liberationist	Radical Liberationist
Organization (continued)	Leadership is exercised by the director	Leadership is exercised by the director with some co-ordination of responsibilities.	Leadership is organized through the co-ordination of various functions.	Leadership is exercised through the combination of situational leaderships.
Methods	Battered women are taken in along with women experiencing all kinds of problems. An individual approach is used.	Group life is encouraged. Individual approach is stressed but some informal group events are organized.	Group approach is important. Group activities are encouraged.	The collective dimensions of the problem take priority over solving personal problems.
	On the basis of their own life experience, non-professional staff provide traditional role model for women.	Personnel is both professional and non-professional. Underlying model is one of professional women helping other women.	Personnel is both professional and non-professional. Underlying model: women gaining independence day-by-day. Attempt is made to define professional competency in new terms.	Personnel is both professional and non-professional. Underlying model: women who are fighting to change the situation and who develop solidarity with other women.

Three levels of operations: — administration — support work — housework	Functional division of labour.	Task sharing with some specialized functions.	Task sharing between staff and residents.
Residents do not participate.	Residents participate.	Residents have ultimate control over decisions.	Process of mutual learning which tends to integrate the residents.
Requests for specialized help concerning administrative procedures and therapeutic treatment.	Personnel training is controlled by specialists and by external resources.	Tendency to view personnel training as a way of working out new approaches to problems in transition houses.	
Salaries determined according to job qualifications and seniority.	Salary varies according to education, seniority and job qualifications.	Equal salaries.	Equal economic situations (on the whole).
Relation to government services: Allow government organizations to define admission criteria.	Relation to government services: Service contracts are concluded which allow a free hand to government services.	Relation to government services: Service contracts are concluded concerning strictly administrative questions.	Relation to government services: Service contracts are kept to a minimum. Collaboration with government institutions is viewed with misgiving.

come together to share common experiences. The woman who seeks refuge in these houses is considered to be in her own home and therefore the staff is not there primarily to serve her. She has a long way to go alone but the staff will be there when times are most difficult. She is informed of her individual as well as collective rights. She can choose to speak out publicly or to get involved in social or political action.

Shifting ideological orientations

It would be misleading, however, to read the foregoing chart as an indication that each house fits snugly into one column or another. The shelters are in flux, continually acting and reacting within the dynamics of the shelter movement as a whole. They exchange ideas, and adopt organizational strategies from each other. At times they are in conflict with each other. At times they co-operate and find points of consensus. Self-help groups are, of necessity, continually changing:

> They are often of a transitory nature (and disappear when the founder(s) of the group resign). They often make significant changes in their objectives as time goes on. This flexibility, an inherent characteristic of grass-roots services, must be respected and every effort should be made to avoid imposing too many administrative norms on them.[32]

Table 2 allows us to suggest certain hypotheses concerning the types of influences and pressures which shape the movement. More conciliatory kinds of leadership tend to come from the legal protectionists and the moderate liberationists principally because they are less extremist. A more protest-oriented leadership comes from the radical liberationists while the pure protectionists tend to represent the forces of inertia.

In a movement as recent as the shelter movement, power is, to some extent, nebulous, up for grabs for those who will use it for the benefit of the movement as a whole. Attempts to further the collective interests of the shelters are, of course, more enriching than efforts which seek to better the lot of some at the expense of others. The overall objectives of the movement are greater than the sum of the interests of each shelter and are sufficiently urgent to encourage collective, unified action.

As the movement's identity becomes clearer, it would not seem desirable that a purely feminist orientation should prevail if this means that other women would drop out. The action of non-feminists can lead to new levels of consciousness and every effort should be made to respect their actions for the particular contribution they make to the movement in general. Adequate analysis can only come from within the movement and should be capable of generating the type of self-criticism necessary to keep the movement dynamic and alive. Above all, it is important that outside influences should not determine the internal debates within the movement.

> ...Sisterhood is not a foregone conclusion. It is possible when one is able to refuse externally defined existence and is able to embrace internally defined existence...[33]

Sisterhood grows from within the model of domestic organization. The only power readily available to women is domestic power, even though some have argued that this is responsibility without power. To the extent that women are conscious of their power, they should seek to share it with other women. A woman who is a victim of violence should not be forced to become a client, guest or beneficiary of someone else. She should simply be seen as a woman who is trying to solve the problem of violence with the support of her sisters. It is important to avoid turning her solely into a recipient of assistance. Ways must be provided which enable her to help others on a day-to-day basis as well.

At the same time, it should be realized that domestic power is a limited form of power which can be an obstacle to exercising broader forms of social power. The shelters must continue to get media attention, they must act as effective pressure groups, and they must develop appropriate means of action in the legal and administrative systems. To share domestic power is only the first step towards developing tools for the struggle for greater social justice in the socio-political system.

The women's shelters should not be content to simply make do within the constraints defined by men. They must burst through these constraints and help create a new society.

Notes

1. See page 98 of this volume.
2. F. L. Paltiel, "Battered Women : concepts, prospects and practices," *Intervention*, Winter 1982, p. 15.
3. Jillian Ridington, "The Transition Process: a feminist environment as reconstitutive milieu," *Victimology: An International Journal*, Vol. 2, 1977-78, p. 565.
4. Marie Lavigne and Yolande Pinard, *Les femmes dans la société québécoise*, Boréal Express, 1977, pp. 208-209.
5. Frédéric Lesemann, *Services and Circuses: Community and the Welfare State*, translated by Lorne Huston and Margaret Heap. Montréal: Black Rose Books, 1984, p. 44.
6. Gilbert Renaud, *L'Éclatement de la profession en service social*, Éd. Saint-Martin, 1978, p. 55.
7. Frédéric Lesemann, *op. cit.*, p. 49.
8. Diane Bélanger and Lucie Rozon, *Les religieuses au Québec*, Libre Expression, 1982, p. 245.
9. *Ibid.*, p. 109.
10. Louise Vandelac, *L'Italie au féminin*. Paris : Éd. Tierce, 1978, p. 142.
11. Brigitte Studer, "Le travail social et les femmes," *Champ social*. Paris: Maspero, 1976, pp. 171-172.
12. Betty Friedan, *The Feminine Mystique*. New York: Dell, 1977, p. 24.
13. Association féminine d'éducation et d'action sociale (women's society for education and social action).
14. *La Gazette des femmes*, Vol. 3, No. 5, December, 1981.
15. It is absurd, of course, to create an artificial barrier between housewives and feminists as if housewives could not be feminists or as if feminists could somehow escape domestic labour. Strictly speaking, one cannot compare a social status (housewives) with a form of political consciousness (feminism). On the other hand,

this distinction has practical usefulness when considering differences in daily practice.
16. Laffont, *La Libération de la femme,* Grammont, Des grands thèmes, p. 11.
17. Jillian Ridington, *op. cit.,* p. 564.
18. *Ibid.,* p. 563.
19. *Ibid.,* p. 564.
20. M. Carrier and D. Grenier, *La Presse,* March 31, 1982.
21. Erin Pizzey, *Scream Quietly or the Neighbours Will Hear.* Harmonsdsworth, England: Penguin Books, 1974, p. 9.
22. Transition House, *A Study of Battered Women,* Vancouver, 1976, p. 7-8.
23. Hélène David, *Analyse socio-économique de la ménagère québécoise.* Montréal: Centre de recherche sur la femme, 1972, p. 156.
24. *Ibid.,* p. 157.
25. William Ryan, *Blaming the Victim.* New York: Vintage Books, revised edition, 1976, p. 8.
26. Congrès du Regroupement provincial des maisons d'hébergement et de transition pour femmes en difficulté (Congress of the Provincial Coalition of Shelters and Transition Houses for Women in Difficulty), Montréal, June 5-6, 1982. Working paper 5, p. 23.
27. Diane Lamoureux, "Mouvement social et lutte des femmes," *Sociologie et sociétés, op. cit.,* p. 134.
28. *Ibid.*
29. A Masi Dale, *Organizing for Women,* Lexington Books, 1981, p. 108.
30. *Ibid.*
31. Diane Lamoureux, *op. cit.,* p. 135.
32. Jérôme Guay, "L'intervenant social face à l'aidant naturel," *Santé Mentale au Québec,* Vol. VII, No. 1, p. 25.
33. Christiane Olivier, *Les Enfants de Jocaste.* Paris: Denoel/Gonthier, 1980, p. 70.

CONCLUSION

The women's shelter movement is shaped and moulded by the relationship between men and women in society. The domination and violence inherent in this relationship is the fundamental reason why the shelters came into being and tried to provide an alternative to official services. This first phase of the shelters movement was vibrant with a sense of urgency as women set about trying to respond to a need which proved far greater than any had imagined. The overwhelming response of women who were victims of violence shattered old misconceptions and led to the creation of more shelters, new policy measures, and finally a network of shelters in all regions of Québec. The volunteer efforts which the first wave of women provided was directed towards understanding the problems involved, developing ways to provide effective, direct help to the victims, and trying to focus public attention on this issue.

Within a very short time, however, semi-professional help began replacing non-professional help in the shelters. Non-professional help had been provided on a volunteer basis within the framework of a peer relationship (between women) and was related to a 'cause' defending specific values. In comparison, semi-professional help was provided by salaried employees within the framework of a therapeutic (helper/helped) relationship. The rights of employees were defined, therapeutic techniques were developed, and a new sector in the job market was created. The common objectives of these two types of situations, however, was to provide a response to a need which was being ignored by society and to help women make personal and social changes concerning the question of violence.

As we now enter a new phase, all kinds of speculation is possible. Certain underlying tendencies, however, indicate the general direction of future developments. The survival of the network of women's shelters depends upon the possibility of working out some kind of synthesis between the non-professional and semi-professional approaches. Development has been so rapid in the shelters that they have not been able to completely absorb the impact of the basic postulates of professional practice and have not fully worked through the ways in which this type of practice influences their relationship with the women seeking refuge. New elements have come into the picture one after another: new techniques, new theories, new government programmes, and it has been impossible to fit these changes together into a coherent whole.

The period of upheaval and tension that many shelters are experiencing at the present time is a reflection of this rapid growth. Non-professional approaches are being tried only in the shelters which have a tradition of innovation and alternative approaches. In the shelters where professional practice is seen as highly desirable, non-professionals are seen as inadequate when viewed according to scientific criteria.

Thus the problem of collaboration between the professions and the shelters remains a thorny one. Gottlieb has noted

> that a productive alliance can be forged between lay persons and professionals so long as there exists an equal partnership and a meaningful exchange of resources.[1]

Other observers who have studied the question of grass-roots support networks are less optimistic:

> ...certain professionals are tempted to dominate certain groups or make them conform to standards of their profession.[2]

Others have pointed out the dangers involved:

> In certain situations, however, the professional is fully aware of the enormous potential of the 'natural' helper and is severely tempted to harness this potential for his own purposes. This leads to a situation of exploitation or what is called co-optation. Experience has shown that the natural helper loses much of his effectiveness when removed from the natural environment or when he is called upon to help someone that he would not normally have chosen to help. A kind of ecological approach must be adopted in a situation like this which respects the reality of natural help without trying to change it or redirect it towards other goals.
> I have been forced to direct much of my energy towards protecting informal groups from what I would call the benevolent imperialism of the State.[3]

When the state tries to impose a certain type of client in the name of making services more efficient or fosters certain techniques or programmes which are far removed from the original objectives of the group of women who set up the shelters, the most probable result is destruction of the vibrant enthusiasm which made it possible to create and run the shelters in the face of impossible odds.

Whatever shortcoming can be imputed to the women's shelters, it must not be forgotten that for a long time they were the only voice which spoke out on the issue of violence against women. The fact that now, certain specialists are presenting learned papers on the subject can never change this fact. Perhaps a judge can do more in less time for women who are victims of violence than the hundreds of anonymous women who volunteer their efforts day in and day out, but he can do nothing without these women. The greatest merit of these shelters is their steadfast conviction that their efforts are necessary if the oppressive structures of society are to be changed.

Notes

1. B. H. Gottlieb, "Informal Support Systems and Helping Networks in Canadian Society," *Canada's Mental Health,* Vol. 29, No. 1, March 1981, p. 2.
2. J. M. Romeder, *Canada's Mental Health, ibid.*, p. 12.
3. Jérôme Guay, "L'intervenant social face à l'aidant naturel," *Santé Mentale au Québec*, Vol. VII, No. 1, p. 26.

Appendix 1

Guide to Dealing with Domestic Violence

First of all, tell someone you trust about the situation (a member of your family, a friend, a neighbour) so that you can get a better perspective on the situation and try to judge the degree of danger involved. If this person does not seem to understand how serious the situation is, contact a welfare office, a community clinic, a journalist, or a women's shelter.

Secondly, get in touch with a lawyer or a legal aid clinic. The law provides protection against mental and physical cruelty. Insist on getting advice as to what to do to protect you and your children.

Prepare ahead of time for the next crisis. Identify a place where you can make an urgent telephone call and where you can go with the children. Figure out a way to avoid the worst and to protect yourself against direct violent outbursts. Do not wait until the last minute to leave and take action. Do not hesitate to leave your home when things become violent.

Have a doctor examine and make a report on any bruises or injuries and contact a lawyer as soon as possible to obtain an order as to separation of bed and board.

Appendix 2

List, by Region, of Women's Shelters in Québec

LOWER ST. LAWRENCE/GASPÉSIE

La Gigogne de Matane	418 562-3377
Maison d'hébergement de Pabos	418 689-6288
La Débrouille de Rimouski	418 724-5067

SAGUENAY/LAC ST-JEAN

Centre féminin du Saguenay à Chicoutimi	418 549-4343
L'Auberge de l'Amitié de Roberval	418 275-4574
Halte Secours de Dolbeau	418 276-3965

QUÉBEC

Maison des femmes de Québec	418 692-4315
Maison Fafard de Baie St-Paul	418 435-2550
Havre des femmes de St-Jean-Port-Joli	418 598-9647
La Gitée de Thetford-Mines	418 335-5551
Havre l'Eclaircie de St-Georges-de-Beauce	418 227-1025
Jonction pour Elle de St-David	418 833-8002

MAURICIE/BOIS-FRANCS

Centre d'hébergement Shawinigan	819 537-8348
L'Entre-Temps de Victoriaville	819 758-6066
La Rose des Vents de Drummond	819 472-5444
Le Toit de l'Amitié de La Tuque	819 523-7829
La Résidence de l'avenue A de Trois-Rivières	819 376-8311

EASTERN TOWNSHIPS

L'Escale de l'Estrie à Sherbrooke	819 569-3611
La Bouée Régionale du Lac-Mégantic	819 583-1233

GREATER MONTRÉAL

Assistance aux Femmes	514 270-8291
Auberge Transition	514 481-0496
Multi-femmes	514 523-1095
Escale pour Elle	514 351-3374
Maison du Réconfort	514 932-9171
Le Prélude de Laval	514 682-3050
Secours aux Femmes	514 727 6871

West Island Women's Shelter	514 620-4845
Interval	514 933-8488
La Dauphinelle	514 253-1224
Parados	514 637-3529
Secours aux Femmes (immigrantes)	514 727-6871
Maison d'hébergement d'Anjou	514 351-6134

LAURENTIANS/LANAUDIÈRE

La Traverse de Joliette	514 759-5882
Le Mitan de Ste-Thérèse	514 435-3651
L'Ombr'Elle de Ste-Agathe	514 326-1321
La Passe-r-elle des Hautes Laurentides	819 623-1523

MONTRÉAL/SOUTH SHORE

L'Accueil de Valleyfield	514 371-4618
La Clé sur la Porte	514 774-1843
Le Coup d'Elle de St-Jean-sur-Richelieu	514 346-1645
Horizon pour Elle de Cowansville	514 263-5046
Carrefour pour Elle de Longueuil	514 651-5800
La Source de Sorel	514 743-2821

OUTAOUAIS

Centre Mechtilde de Hull	819 777-2952
Maison Unies-Vers-Femmes de Gatineau	819 568-4710

NORTH SHORE

Maison des femmes de la Côte-Nord (Baie-Comeau/Hauterive)	418 296-4733

Le Centre des Femmes de Forestville   418 587-2533

NORTHWEST

Alternative pour Elles de Rouyn   819 797-1754
Maison Mikana d'Amos   819 732-9161
Le Nid de Val d'Or   819 825-3865

More books from **BLACK ROSE BOOKS**

FEMINISM IN CANADA

From Pressure to Politics

edited by Angela Miles and Geraldine Finn

This collection brings together for the first time the writings of Canada's leading feminist scholars. It launches an incisive critique of traditional academic thought and how it complements and sustains male values in our society. It is a book which bridges the gap between scholarship and the women's movement, raising fundamental questions of theory and practice.

Contributors include: Mary O'Brien, Margaret Benston, Jill McCalla Vickers, Jeri Dawn Wine, Madeleine Gagnon, Patricia Hughes, Ruth Pierson, Alison Prentice, Helen Levine, Carole Yawney, Yolande Cohen, Geraldine Finn, Angela Miles and Marjorie Cohen.

315 pages
Paperback ISBN: 0-919619-00-2 $12.95
Hardcover ISBN: 0-919619-02-9 $22.95
Women/Politics

MOTHER WAS NOT A PERSON

edited by Margret Andersen

2nd Edition

"A diversified compilation, **Mother** should be read by all those interested in the feminist movement and especially by those curious to know of the specifics concerning the movement in Quebec. Teachers wishing to incorporate into their civilization courses the history and evolution of the women's movement in the francophonic world will find this Canadian publication a valuable source of information."
Prof. Anthony Caprio
Lehman College, SUNY

This book is an anthology of writings by Montréal women. It deals with the politics, poetry, educational and related dimensions of women in our society. It is mandatory reading for the general public in Canada, as we are flooded with books on women from the USA.

274 pages
Paperback ISBN: 0-919618-00-6 $7.95
Hardcover ISBN: 0-919618-12-X $16.95
Women/Sociology

Send for complete free catalogue

3981 boul. St-Laurent
Montréal, Québec
H2W 1Y5

Printed by
the workers of
Editions Marquis, Montmagny, Québec
for
Black Rose Books Ltd.